Remembering G

Makeda Silvera

Sister Vision

Black Women and Women of Colour Press

ISBN 0-920813-60-7

Canadian Cataloguing in Publication Data

Silvera, Makeda. 1955-
Remembering G and other stories

ISBN 0-920813-60-7

I. Title.

PS8587.I55R4 1991   C813'.54   C91-094440-7
PR9199.3.855R4 1991

Cover & Book Design: Stephanie Martin
Typesetting: Blackbird Design Collective
Printed and bound in Canada by union labour

Published by   Sister Vision Press
                 P.O. Box 217
                 Station E
                 Toronto, Ontario
                 Canada M6H 4E2

The author wishes to express her gratitude to the Ontario Arts Council for its generous support during the writing of this book and to the Toronto Arts Council.

To my daughters Ayoola and Keisha
For keeping the memory alive

Stephanie
for taking the journey with me

Sharon
for your spirit and energy

Table of Contents

Acknowledgements

My thanks to Patricia K. Murphy and Stephanie Martin for editing
and detailed comments and criticism throughout the development.
My grandmother Lucille Johnson and mother, Joy Thorpe for their
support and for some of the details of the book.

An additional thanks to Stephanie Martin for coping with my
computer phobia; and her ear for the natural rythmn of our Jamaican
nation language.

No Beating Like Dis One

"**No** beating like dis one, a sorry fi yuh!" My cousin, Elithia, taunting me as I waited for Auntie Maggie to get dressed to deliver me personally to Mama. She was taking no chance in sending a note with me. No, this news was too important, too juicy to give me to deliver. Auntie Maggie wanted to be there to dramatise, to show me up like some piece of dutty cloth.

I spent two weekends out of every month at Auntie Maggie's house. I can't say I enjoyed them very much, except for the company of Winnifred, my other cousin, who also spent weekends with Auntie Maggie. Her house was larger and had more rooms than our two houses combined. And there was Lloydie. He was thirteen years old and lived next door with his mother in a rented room.

Auntie Maggie's daughter, Elithia, was nine. She was short and chubby, with equally short, stubby hair parted in countless plaits. She hated them, especially the way Auntie Maggie always tied pieces of ribbons at the end. Whenever Auntie Maggie was out of earshot we would chant, "Picky-picky head, go buy new head."

Friday and Saturday evenings we would play games. I was not very good at marbles, but I loved to watch Winnifred play with Lloydie. Winnifred was good. We played hopscotch and jacks, but my favourites were baseball and dandy-shandy. Elithia liked these two games best. I was always eager to include Elithia, because she wasn't a good player and I would drive the ball into her back or belly, laughing wickedly when she bent over in pain.

Elithia was Auntie Maggie's only daughter. Her mouth was as big and loud as a petchary bird and she loved to take news to Auntie Maggie. If we excluded her from a game, she would threaten to tell Auntie Maggie about something that happened weeks ago that the rest of us had long forgotten. We would then be banned from playing with Lloydie or from sitting on the verandah in the evenings.

"No beating like dis one." Elithia's mean voice sing-songing behind my ears. I tried not to cry, not because I was thinking about the beating I would get when I got home, but because I couldn't hit blabbermouth Elithia right where she deserved it. I couldn't even promise her, Auntie Maggie was right beside me. "Come we ready, mek we go."

I burned with embarrassment. I would have to take the bus with Auntie Maggie. Auntie Maggie was fat. Very fat. The few times I'd ridden the bus with Auntie Maggie she'd used up all of two seats. Everyone would stare at us. I loved Auntie Maggie, despite her exaggerated accounts of what I did. I just didn't like taking the bus with her. And today Uncle Blue, her husband, was not around to take us in his car.

I reached the bus stop with Auntie Maggie, with Elithia's soppy voice still singing in my ear. "No beating like dis one. No beating like dis one."

I remembered the last time I got a beating....

Congregational Hall School was about six miles from home, in downtown Kingston and close to the higglers and their guava cheese and grater cakes. We would spend our bus fare on sweets and then beg from people at the bus stop. Who could resist, "Come buy piece a guava cheese, only trupence!" "Nice girl wid de pretty ribbon, greater cake fi only a treepence. And dem fresh!" "Paradise plums fi sale. Pretty girl wid de nice hair—over here!"

Almost every evening I spent my bus fare on one of those tempting sweets. After sucking the last taste from my tongue, I would set out to get threepence to get me home on the bus. Two days a week I also visited my father at his barbershop on East Queen Street, not far from Parade Station. Papa rarely came to our avenue and he was always glad to see me. He would greet me with a big hug and boast to his customers, "Yes man, dis is my daughter from my second marriage. Four from de first marriage and two little outside one. And dem all look like me."

The customers in turn would express their admiration. Then my father would give me an ice cream cone or sometimes bun and cheese. After eating, I would ask for threepence to pay my bus fare. I had to be careful about this because he was always quick to blame Mama. "She didn't give yuh enough fi yuh bus fare? I'll have to come up dat avenue and have a good talk wid her." When Papa was in that mood I would say goodbye and head for Parade Station.

Mama knew I visited him sometimes but certainly not as often as twice a week. If she'd known I visited him to beg bus fare, she would have beat the living daylights out of me. It happened before: "From de day dat man walk out, he never even try to find out if ah have nuff to feed you. Never ask about money fi school uniform and yuh gone to beg him trupence, gal?"

"Please m'am, beg yuh a trupence to tek de bus home." Or "Good evening, mama. Beg yuh a bus fare please?" Sorrowful and lost.

The lady would ask, "What 'appen to yuh money?" And I would whimper, "Ah lost it, m'am," or "Someone tek it out of my school bag, m'am." If it seemed she was undecided, I would continue, "What time is it, m'am? Jesus! Ah didn't know it was so late! Ah should have been home to pick up my little sister, poor ting. She must be still out at de piazza hungry and waiting fi me."

I was a loner at this and if I came down to Parade with a friend from school, we would be very careful to do our begging in separate directions. Some days I would get the threepence on my first try. Some days it took a long time to get the money or I would only get twopence. Those evenings I walked home, always following the bus route, the long way home, but the only one I knew. Walk up Parade, past the big Coronation Market, on to Spanish Town Road, past deserted and burned-down buildings, past shacks, burial grounds, madman, madwoman, children in tear-up clothes, on to Waltham Park Road, then finally Chisholm Avenue and then the turn onto our little avenue.

The day I got the beating of my life was a Friday evening. I begged and begged at Parade but couldn't come up with threepence. I decided not to go to Papa, afraid he would accompany me home. That Friday I begged for hours. When the last lady I tried told me it was six o'clock I knew it was time to start walking home. I began the long walk, munching on my guava cheese and thinking about what excuse to give Mama for being so late.

Mama greeted me at the gate, "Weh yuh deh since school let out?" As I opened my mouth to answer, her right hand came down on my face. I fell on the ground, then got to my feet quick and ran to the shed in the back of the yard. Mama sat waiting on the verandah. It was dark by then and I was hungry and frightened. Why didn't she call me or shout at me? I tried to slip by her into the house. Tamarind switch came down on my back and Mama gripped the collar of my blouse.

"Yuh won't stop eat off yuh bus fare? Yuh won't stop beg 'pon street? Yuh love call down disgrace 'pon me? Tek dis."

The tamarind switch danced all over my back. I was shaking and screaming. The next-door neighbours opened their windows to hear better. Some came to the fence to get a better look. Mama didn't let up. "Yuh want to call down de whole avenue?"

"No, Mama."

"Well shut yuh mout. Yuh no have no shame gal?"

Throughout all the talking, Mama did not miss a beat. My back was the African drum she never knew. I continued to scream, yelling for the police. This was a sign of disrespect. "Is show yuh want to show me up gal? Is scandal yuh want to call down on de yard?"

I don't remember when it ended. What stayed with me for a long time were the welts and cuts on my back and behind. It was a long, long time before I begged at Parade again.

Auntie Maggie and I sat at the very back of the bus. "When ah done tell Lulu what yuh going on wid, yuh going to be sorry! What dat yuh doing at your age, eh? Eleven years old and yuh looking man already!"

The whole bus load of people turned round to look at me. Auntie Maggie had a full house for the dress rehearsal and when we got home she would give a perfect performance.

Soon the entire bus was taking part. "Yuh have to watch dem pickney nowadays. Dem get big before dem time," a red, freckle-faced woman offered.

Another nudged the young girl seated next to her, "Yuh hear dat? Yuh watch yuh step. Cause anyhow yuh do a ting like dat, a bruk yuh foot."

An old woman announced, "She need a good beating."

From the front a hard-faced woman was quick to add,"Yuh have to stop dem tings before dem reach higher proportion. 'Fore yuh know it, she bring in belly." They talked around me like flies swarming a plate of food.

People got off the bus, new people came on. Auntie Maggie continued her recitation and the new people on the bus took up the chorus.

"Yes m'am, me know a girl who start out jus' like dat, de same womanish style. She now sixteen and is tree pickney she have fi tree different man."

"She start see her menstruation yet?" a tall man with glasses asked.

"No not yet. Ah tekking her home to talk to my sister. Mek sure she get a real beating." One man in the bus eyed me up and down.

By now I was crying. The voices went on. "And look 'pon her

eye. See how dem bright. Yuh can tell she bad."

More agreement. "Yes, especially when dem start fi cry, dat is a sure sign of badness." Another time I hadn't cried and the public complaint was that I was dried-eyed and womanish.

I had everyone's attention. Nobody was paying attention to Auntie Maggie's size. Even I forgot that Auntie Maggie took up two entire seats at the back of the bus.

"Chisholm Avenue," the conductress called out. Auntie Maggie said goodbye to the crowd and pushed me to the front. Everybody I knew was on the street that evening. I put on my don't-talk-to-me face as I passed my friends, but that didn't help.

"What 'appen?"

"How come yuh Auntie holding on to yuh so tight?"

"Yuh going to get a beating?"

"Yuh coming to Tony birthday party tomorrow?"

Auntie Maggie didn't miss that. "She not coming to nobody party. De only party she going to is de one in her bed. Yuh wait till ah tell her mother what a good-for-nutting daughter she have. She won't see de light of de day fi de rest of her life."

"What she do, m'am?" a fat, round-faced girl named Joy asked. My heart jumping all over my chest and sweat covering my face, I waited for Auntie Maggie to go on and on as she had in the bus, but she didn't seem to hear Joy's question.

"Yuh wait till yuh go home and Lulu hear about your carrying on. All dis shame a little pickney like yuh bring down on yuh mother. Want to turn big 'oman before yuh time."

What would it be? Worse than the Parade beating? Mama's heavy hands? The tamarind switch?

Joy, Tony, Babes, Petal, Rowan, Glory and two boys I didn't know were now trailing behind us. A tall, heavy-set boy joined the procession. It was Joy's older brother, singing, "Fatty walking down de road with a skinny girl in hand. Little girl, where yuh going to run to, oh yeah."

Auntie Maggie stopped to give him a big cut eye. He added more verses and followed us straight to the gate of my yard. Auntie

Maggie, grabbing onto my wrist, commanded me to walk faster. When I protested, "Auntie, ah walking as fast as ah can," she gave me one cuff on my forehead and told me not to backtalk.

The procession laughed and danced behind us. Joy's brother added new verses. Auntie Maggie's face was purpling up. Despite her fingernails digging into my wrist, I had to bite my lips not to laugh.

"Girl, yuh auntie fat, eh. Hey mama, what should ah eat to have a nice round figure like yuh, mama?" The others laughed and applauded.

Auntie turned on me, "Is where yuh know dem hooligans from?" With this she let go of my wrist to twist my right ear until I was sure she'd torn it off. I was beyond shame. I screamed and cried and I didn't care who saw me.

By the time we turned off Chisholm and onto my avenue the crowd had doubled. I no longer cared about any beating. So what if Mama tied me up with a rope against the tamarind tree and beat me till the next day.

Mama was sitting on the verandah, reading the newspaper when we reached the house. Auntie Maggie pushed me forward, stopping to latch the gate behind her. Part of the crowd waited at the gate, others ran next door to Joy's yard.

"Lulu, dis girl of yours going to mek yuh shame before she turn thirteen, yuh nuh. Ah don't know what yuh going to do with her."

Mama picked up her knitting. I stood in front of them, my knees wobbling.

"Sit down." Mama motioned to me.

"Is dese tings mek her tink she is a big woman, yuh know. Yuh should let her stand still until we finish talking."

Mama ignored Auntie Maggie and told her to start at the beginning.

"Lulu, ah don't even know where to start. Ah know yuh going to shame, my dear sister, but dis girl of yours don't have any of dat. Ah in de backyard dis morning washing clothes and beg her to go buy some soapsud at de shop fi me. Ah wait and ah wait and she don't come back. Anyway, ah give her de benefit of de doubt. Yuh know dat is Saturday and de line-up at de shop long. Winnifred and Freddy was inside dusting de furniture, so ah send little Elithia to put her head out de gate and look if she see dis one coming."

With this Auntie Maggie paused, took out her handkerchief, wiped her big round face. "Girl, go and get me a glass of water. Put nuff ice in it." She stopped the story while I went to get her ice water.

"Well, little Elithia come go out to de gate and look up and down de road and no sight of dis one. She come and tell me dis. Ah wait a while longer and ah worried now, so ah send her back to look again. When she come back, ah say to her, 'Elithia, go cross de road and knock on Lloydie mother gate and find out if dey see her."

Auntie Maggie stopped to fan her face with a piece of Mama's newspaper and continued, "Lulu, ah hear de gate bang loud and say, 'What 'appen, Elithia?' Not a word come from de little girl mout."

Auntie Maggie got up, stretched her legs and commented on the tree laden with ackees. "As ah was saying Lulu, not a word from Elithia mout. So ah say to her, 'Yuh find her?' and she say, 'Yes, Mommy.' Ah say, 'Where?' and she say, 'She and Lloydie on Lloydie mother veran-dah.'"

Auntie Maggie stopped again. By now I was getting tired of the story, tired of Auntie Maggie. I felt like grabbing the story out her mouth and telling it myself, getting my beating and going to bed.

Mama kept knitting. I couldn't read her face. Waiting for Mama to say something, Auntie Maggie took a sip of water and wiped her face again with her handkerchief.

Mama looked up. "Maggie, ah don't know de story so tell me what 'appen. It must be important if yuh tek bus all de way here to tell me."

Auntie Maggie got up from her chair and arms akimbo, looked at me and then at Mama. "Sister, ah don't know what yuh going to do wid dis girl."

"Maggie, yuh already say dat. Continue with de story," Mama cut in, this time a slight edge to her voice.

Auntie Maggie ignored that and went on, "By de time she catch twelve is living trouble yuh going to have on yuh hand. Dis girl is a risk. When she start to menstruate yuh will have to keep her tie up to avoid shame an disgrace on dis avenue."

Mama kept knitting, looking directly at the centrepiece she was working on for the dining table. The zinc fence separating our yard from Joy's sagged with people waiting to hear what Auntie Maggie would say next.

"Well, me sister. Elithia went over de yard and when she see what she see on de verandah she run and come tell me. She didn't let dis one know she see her."

"Maggie, me daughter have a name. Use it. She don't name 'Dis One.'"

"Lord, it hot." Auntie Maggie fanned the air viciously. "When Elithia tell me what she see ah couldn't believe it. Ah nearly box her mout, but ah know my Elithia don't tell lies, and she wouldn't mek up someting like dat. She don't have dat dirtiness in her mind to tink up dose kind of ting.

"Jesus, it hot," she went on to no one in particular. "Ah hope it rain. We need it, everyting so dry."

I thought the fence was about to fall as people jostled for a better view. "Yuh ackee tree full, eh Lulu," Auntie Maggie said. "A wouldn't mind a dozen or so to tek home. B really like ackee. Your yard really blessed, all dese fruitful trees. Ah have a big yard and...."

Mama cut in, "Ah just pick a few dozens off de tree dis morning. Yuh can tek dem home with yuh."

"God bless you, Lulu. Now where was I in de story? Oh yes. Little Elithia carry me to de spot on de verandah where she and Lloydie was. When ah come and look ah frighten. As dere is a heaven and a God Lulu, ah never know dis girl so ripe, so womanish."

Auntie Maggie stopped her account and kicked off her shoes. The smell from her feet was overpowering, but she didn't seem to notice and Mama didn't comment. I tried to breathe through my mouth.

"Yes Lulu, as ah was saying, when ah see dem it was a sight dat would mek even Satan blush." She got up and spit in one of the flowerpots on the verandah. I looked at Mama. Mama's face was the same. The only response was more shuffling against the zinc fence.

"Lulu, when ah tiptoe and look on de verandah, on de cold concrete, ah see dis shameface girl lie down and dutty Lloydie right on top of her. Her skirt lift high over her face." Auntie Maggie looked at Mama in amazement.

Mama was still knitting. She hadn't said a word. "Wait Lulu, yuh don't hear what ah just say to you. Dutty bwoy Lloydie was laying down on top of dis one, in de broad daylight on de verandah, on de cold concrete tiles."

The zinc fence swayed back and forth.

Finally Mama spoke. "So dem was naked?"

Auntie Maggie looked at her in disbelief. "Yuh wasn't listening to me Lulu? Ah say her frock was over her head. Him still had him pants and shoes on, but de fact of de matter is dat dem know what dem was doing. And who knows, if ah didn't catch dem in time, dey would be stark naked."

"Is no example fi little Elithia, yuh know. Dis chile is evil and is no good fi a girl chile to be growing up with so much woman-ness in her already."

"Well," said Mama, "Ah going to mek sure she don't corrupt Elithia any more."

"How dat?" Auntie Maggie asked, totally confused.

"Ah won't send her around any more."

Mama motioned to me to go have a bath. It was almost night though the sun was still out. I didn't hear any more of the conversation and Auntie Maggie finally left with her ackees.

I sat in my bath wondering what would it be? A piece of wire from the electric light pole? The big leather belt that hung behind the bedroom door? Mama called "come eat". I finished everything on my plate.

Mama spoke again, "Clean your teeth when yuh finish eat, come kiss mi goodnight and say yuh prayers before yuh go to bed."

The sun was slowly going to sleep.

The Funeral

I knew about duppies and rolling calves even before I went to my first funeral. So when grandfather died in 1964, I knew he would eventually turn into a duppy.

We called him grandpa, he was a gentle, soft-spoken man with a long, white beard. He always found time to play with us kids, always had a hand of green banana or a piece of yam to give to the less fortunate; so I knew that he wouldn't come back in the form of a rolling calf to haunt me. But when Mama told me I would have to spend the night with Granny in the very same bed that Grandpa died in, I was afraid. On top of that, it just didn't seem fair that my cousins would have the room with the big iron bed and the mattress thrown on the wooden floor.

Granny tried to calm my nerves by suggesting that she would sleep on grandpa's side, but that didn't matter much to me, my nine year old imagination was on the run.

'Black duppy dress up in a white clothes.' 'Duppy wid out face or head just two long foot, high on sticks.'

Granny tried to comfort me by hugging me tight in her big arms and telling me an anancy story, but I pulled away from her, stiff with fear that I might smell the dead on her.

A whole month of darkness surrounded me before I fell asleep in the hot, muggy, two room, wooden house in the hills of Port Maria. But it was a restless sleep and I felt Granny throwing my legs and arms to the other side of the bed, my legs echoing against the wooden walls of the house.

That night grandpa came to me in a dream. He had all his duppy friends with him. They were happy, laughing, pointing fingers at the living in judgement. The duppies were all dressed in white from head to toe. They scared me with their wild laughter and white cloth draped around them for cover. They had long nails and long, yellow teeth and danced to mad music.

Grandpa kept calling me to come and join them, but I was too frightened. One woman duppy smiled at me and curled up her long fingernails, beckoning to me to come. But I knew I didn't belong and waved regretfully to Grandpa. The dream had almost faded when a whole set of rolling calves attacked. Grandpa ran away, far out of reach of the rolling calves.

The rolling calves looked nothing like the duppies. Where the duppies had two feet, the rolling calves were four-footed beasts, with red eyes and smoke and fire coming out of their mouths and big bells clanging around their necks. Nobody told me to cover my ears, but I knew that if I listened to the ring of the bell it would drive me crazy, and if I didn't shield my eyes form the fire in theirs, I could be blinded, or worse still, turned into a rolling calf.

I must have screamed and hollered and kicked and rolled because I was awakened by a cold pot of water. My aunts and cousins were all standing over me. I tried to explain the dream and they all nodded with understanding. I was sure they didn't understand. One of my aunts fitted me into one of Granny's old blouses and spread a piece of plastic on my water-soaked side of the mattress.

Day light was just peeping out and I, who usually slept late, jumped up when I turned over and felt Granny missing from the bed. My cousins were still asleep, but outside the men form Jarvis corner were already digging grandpa's grave. I felt cold watching them. G was coming in from Kingston later that day to build the coffin. My uncles had already chopped down two cotton trees to use as wood for the coffin. Grandpa would be buried on the property, some miles away from the house.

The house, the outdoor kitchen, the steps and the yard were crowded with friends and neighbours. Mama said it would get more crowded during the evening when the wake began. There would be a lot more people every night, drinking and talking until Grandpa was buried.

Then she explained that on the ninth night there would be a long set up until morning with even more people singing, drinking, eating and talking about grandpa.

"Dat is call de nine-night. Dem drink and eat and sing whole heap of hymn, sometime dem so drunk from de rum dat dem talk pure foolishness...but is nine-night dat, and a final farewell to de dead."

Everything Mama said was true. The men and the women who were around talked for hours about Grandpa, what he was like as a boy, how he met Granny and on and on. They played dominoes and cards and ate bread and fried sprat and drank rum all night. I fell asleep outside on a Coco-Cola box, afraid to go into the bed.

As the funeral day got closer, more relatives arrived from Canada, England and the United States. Most I was meeting for the first time. The first two days they were around, I couldn't stand their sweet, syrupy voices. Always going on about how big we had grown. Who we looked like, or didn't look like. Who had long hair and who had good hair. Who was lighter than who. Whose nose was straighter than whose. But I liked it when Granny's wooden floor had another mattress thrown on it and there were more people in the room at night.

The day of the funeral we were all lined up outside of Grandpa's little tool shed, where his body had been stored for the last five days packed with blocks of ice to keep it from rotting. We had come to bid our farewell, but Mama, Auntie Maggie, Aunt May and grannie forced my cousins and I to watch them dress Grandpa. Mama and Auntie Maggie unwrapped Grandpa from the three white sheets banded around him and removed the ice from his body. My cousin Elithia ran from the shed and hid under the bed. The others looked on and sometimes covered their eyes. I watched as he was washed and dried. They put him in clean, starched, white underpants, a white shirt, navy blue pants and his navy blue jacket to match. Mama sent one of my older cousins to get the scissors and then Mama cut the pockets from Grandpa's navy blue jacket. His face and chest a sea of Johnson's baby powder, he lay there as if he had drank too much rum the night before. G and two men came soon after to lift grandpa and place him inside his coffin lined with white cloth. Mama and Auntie Maggie carefully lifted the dead-water they bathed Grandpa in and threw it some distance behind the shed. They warned us not to walk in it, or go near.

It was time for us to get dressed. I washed outside in a big zinc tub behind granny's house, then put on my lavender dress that John had made some time ago but which still looked new, my white socks and black patent shoes that I wore to St. Luke's church on Sundays. It was hard for me to believe that we were all getting so dressed up only to bury Grandpa not so far from the house in his own yard.

My grandparents house sat on over ten acres of land with banana, ackee, coconut and breadfruit trees. Fruit trees of every variety and ground provisions like yam, coco and dasheen.

I stayed behind to help granny into her girdle and brassiere. Mama, by now dressed in a black dress with matching black hat and shoes, was fussing over granny's hair.

"Granny, remember to put on de panties," Mama reminded. "Remember it have to be black and yuh have to wear black for de next six months."

The yard was crowded when I came out of the house. People from all over Jarvis corner, Port Maria and as far as St. Ann's and Kingston came to say goodbye to Grandpa. We walked over to the grave side with our Bibles in hand, my black patent shoes sinking deep into the black dirt. There was crying and wailing even before the parson began to preach. Some people had even started to drink from early in the morning, and one man who claimed to be a childhood friend of grandpa, had to be held on to tight by two other mourners. "Grandpa, grandpa," he called out, "ah coming wid yuh, mek space fe me in yuh grave."

Auntie Maggie pushed a handkerchief in Granny's hands and whispered something to her. Suddenly the mourners grew quiet, even grandpa's childhood friend. We all watched as Granny tore the handkerchief in half, putting a piece in her brassiere and the rest in Grandpa's grave.

"Dis is de last ah we," she said dramatically. 'Stay weh yuh deh, me and yuh done. Yuh gone weh. Keep to yuh way and I keep to mine."

She finished with a scream, summoning the other mourners to resume bawling and crying. It seemed the funeral went on for hours before grandpa was finally laid in the big, deep, black hole. Granny fainted and had to be lifted and carried back to her bed. Mama and Auntie Maggie gave her smelling salts and she came back to life. I was standing by the door watching, afraid that Granny would die too and I would have to go to another funeral and sleep in another dead bed and watch Granny get dressed for her own burial.

"Yuh did remember to cut out de pocket from him jacket?" Aunt May asked granny. She said yes, she had already done that.

Mama cut in. "Yes and we must also put up a big mirror right at de door of dis room and in de other room too." I listened for an explanation to all this, but there was none.

The women and men were still in the yard drinking, singing, talking and eating bread and fish. I asked Mama when we would leave for Kingston. With grandpa buried not too far from the house, I didn't want to have any more dreams about duppies and rolling calves, but Mama said we would have to wait until after the ninth night.

There were more days and nights of people talking about the dead, about sickness, about fatal accidents, about still-born babies, crib death and of duppies and rolling calves.

The preparation for the nine-night outdid everything else I'd

seen since I'd been in Port Maria. Mama, Auntie Maggie, Aunt May
and the other women took over the cooking. There were platters of
fried chicken and fried sprat, roast pork, fish soup, green bananas and
big pots of white rice.

G was in charge of getting the cask rum in a big barrel from a rum
shop some distance away. Mama said I could go with him. I was glad
to be out of that dead yard with all its talk of illness and terrible
things. I walked for some time but then my feet got tired and G lifted me onto his back and sang and told me stories the rest of the way
to the rum shop.

On our way back I decided to ask him some questions that I was
afraid to ask anyone else. "G, why dem throw de dead-water so far
from the house, and why Mama seh we cyaan walk in it?"

"Dem seh dat if you walk in de water used to wash de dead you
will get ulcer and small pox and die soon after."

"G, why dem cut de pockets out of Grandpa's jacket?"

"So dat when him turn duppy, him won't come back wid stones
in his pocket to stone granny."

"I thought only rolling calf did dat kind of a ting."

"Well..." said G, "well...de rolling calf could capture de duppy to
mek him into a rolling calf and den influence him to throw stone at
grannie."

"G, why did Granny tear de kerchief in half and give Grandpa
one piece and she put the other in her brassiere?"

"So dat him won't come back to trouble or haunt her. Duppy
suppose to stay with duppy and de living suppose to mix with only
de living."

"G, why dem want to put mirrors in every room near de doors?"

"Duppy 'fraid to see demself in a mirror, so if duppy see a mirror, duppy won't come into dat room and trouble anybody."

"G what is de nine-night going to be like?"

"The nine-night is when we all say our last goodbye to Grandpa.
We eat whole heap of food, and some a we drink whole heap of rum.
We also sprinkle some of de rum on de dirt in de yard. Dat is for de
good duppies to partake in and welcome grandpa into dere commu-

nity. Den we sing songs of praise for de dead and de rest of de duppies."

"G," I said, "sing one of de songs fi me. I will be fast asleep
when dem start singing tonight."

"Dere is a la-a-and of pu-u-u-re de-e-e-elight, where sa-a-aint
i m-m-m-or-t-a-a-al reign." G stretched out each word, making me
laugh on his back,.

"G..."

"What is it my little princess?"

"G...why is it dat Granny haffi wear black panties for six months?"

"Duppy 'fraid of black. Duppy won't trouble Granny if she in
black. Duppy Grandpa will leave her alone."

"But G why not a black dress, or a black handkerchief? Why
black panties?"

"Come to tink of it," said G, "Ah never thought of dat one. Ask
yuh modder when we get back." By now, we were close to home. I
begged G for more songs and stories wishing this walk would last a
little longer.

Confirmation

For most of the twelve years I lived on my avenue, Jackie Hayes and I were best friends. We lived next door to each other and went to Sunday School together at St. Luke's Anglican Church. Both Mama and Mrs. Hayes rented out rooms to help with the mortgage and between them they had the best flower beds on the street. But the similarities stopped there. Mama didn't live with her husband and she wasn't a professional working women like Mrs. Hayes. And Mama loved to drink rum and read Harlequins.

Mama was a handsome woman, her complexion the colour of dark chocolate fudge and brown eyes like mine. She wore her hair straightened, cut short and brushed back from her face. At five foot two I was almost as tall, but where I was skinny like a nail Mama was shapely. Mama didn't mix much in the company of women, but she talked with everyone on the street. She said she preferred her own company and next to that, the company of men. Mama said, "Give me man company any day. 'Oman chat too much. Dem chat even what dem don't know."

She puzzled the street, especially the women, and they didn't like it when their men friends sat on our verandah with Mama, drinking rum and talking politics. They would say, "She live on dis avenue so long and we really don't even know her," and "She not a full 'oman but half man." I heard most of this from Jackie. She always had something to tell about Mama and I was always eager to hear it, but whenever I figured Jackie was enjoying the latest talk about Mama too much, I would squint my eyes at her, suck my teeth and with my left hand slowly sink my fingernails into her arm. Jackie wouldn't cry, she would just crawl from under our secret place, the house bottom, and run home. She would keep away from me for days, until I went over to apologise. I would promise never to do it again and we would hug, swearing to be best friends forever.

Mama didn't look like half-women half-man to me and I hated it when the women on the street whispered so. I didn't understand. It didn't puzzle me that Mama talked politics, drank white rum like a man, knitted and crocheted, tended her flowerbed and baked the best cakes and sweets that were sold in all the shops in our neighbourhood. But it puzzled me that Mama didn't go to church. She went only to bury the dead, yet she knew the Bible from Genesis to Revelations, and while she baked, she sang with such power and purpose that people stopped to listen. Mama said the spirit of her church was in her heart. I didn't understand what she meant, but I nodded when she told me and didn't question why I had to go to Sunday School.

Jackie had two sisters and a brother. She was the oldest. Her mother was a teacher, her father a bus driver. Her parents had a real stuck-up attitude and none of their children were allowed to play on the street with the rest of us. But every chance she got, Jackie met me under the house bottom to play house, school and doctor.

Sunday afternoons we were in complete charge of ourselves to go to and from Sunday School. Sixpence for our bus fares and three-pence each for the collection plate. Sundays we wore our best clothes to church and Mama let me wear the watch that Auntie Gwen sent me from England and I'd put on my beloved black patent leather shoes. It was also the only day I didn't have to wear my hair in plaits. Instead, Mama brushed it back and tied it with a ribbon.

Most Sundays we held back our collection money to buy sweets after church. If the teacher paid special attention to us we would pretend to drop a coin in the plate and then pass it on to the person next to us. We never made friends at Sunday School. There wasn't time for that and we were never encouraged to talk with other children much.

Miss Patterson, our teacher, was a dried-out, shrivelled-up currant of a woman. And mean. If she caught us whispering or dozing off, she would shout at us.

We didn't go to St. Luke's every Sunday. Some evenings we took the bus through neighbourhoods with big trees, beautiful homes and large spaces to run and play in. We gaped at white and brown children playing outdoors in socks and shoes and riding bicycles. Sometimes we got off the bus and walked through the streets with the big houses. But most times we stayed on the bus, poking each other over the size of the trees, the swings, the bicycles and cars in the driveways.

Our parents never asked us in any detail about Sunday School, so we didn't try to remember passages of the Bible or the themes of the lessons. Mama would say to me "How was Sunday School?" and I would answer, "Fine, Mama."

Many things changed when I was twelve. I started my menstruation, Jackie left for the United States with her family, and it was my confirmation year. "Every girl should be confirmed," said Mama, "because dis can help yuh in all areas of life. When time for yuh to get a job, it can help." I nodded, but I was thinking about Jackie and how much I missed her. I would be going to confirmation lessons by myself.

I started my confirmation lessons on a Friday evening after school. I came out of class not remembering anything about the lesson. My mind had been on the rolling hills behind the church and the pretty flowers waiting to be picked. And Friday evenings in Kingston were full of excitement. Street vendors, higglers, the big

Woolworth's Department Store across from St. Luke's. I didn't plan anything, I just got tired of going to the lessons. I spent one Friday evening walking through Woolworth's and Courts Furniture Store. The next Friday I went to the Tom Redcomb Library and read books. Some Fridays I rode up and down the elevator at Court's. One day I got home in time to hear Mama talking to Miss Gloria, our dressmaker, about my confirmation dress. Time was going and I had already missed several classes. There were only four more lessons before the big ceremony. That night in bed I asked God to forgive me. I went to sleep promising Him that next Friday would see me at class.

Miss Patterson seemed surprised to see me back in classes, but she didn't say anything. I sat quietly, trying to figure out how much I missed. I went to the next class early and asked Miss Patterson for some extra lessons. She gave me a few chapters to study at home. That would make up for my absences. Two weeks before confirmation Miss Patterson read out the names of those to be confirmed. My name wasn't on the list. Must be a mistake, I thought. I waited until everyone had left and then I went over to her as she was packing up her books. She looked up.

"Miss, ah didn't hear mi name call," I said timidly. Miss Patterson said I had missed four classes that were very important and therefore I would not be in this confirmation class. I didn't want to believe her. In front of me I saw Mama's face, the confirmation dress, my white socks and new white shoes Mama was planning to buy for the ceremony. What was I going to tell her?

"Mam, yuh don't understand. Ah have to be in dis confirmation class," I pleaded. "We still have two weeks. Can't yuh give mi some extra lessons fi mi to catch up?"

"I can only go by the rules and follow instructions," Miss Patterson said in a flat voice not at all fitting for a church teacher. I thanked her and turned to leave. She called after me, "The only person who could help is Reverend Matthews and he will be in church on Sunday." I thanked her again and left the church. I went across the street to Woolworth's Department Store and bought a soft drink and to consider my next move. I missed Jackie so much. There was no one I could talk with about this problem. I had to do it all myself.

I remembered passing Reverend Matthews' house with Jackie on one of our Sunday outings, his name big and bold on the gate. Going to see him was the best thing to do.

I took the bus to Reverend Matthews' house. It was mango season and I wished I lived in one of those big houses with the julie mango trees and swings made of iron. A mother and a father with a car. A maid to tend me. I felt so ashamed. I loved my house and Mama, but I couldn't keep myself from comparing those imported iron swings to my rope swing tied to the almond tree. G had bought the rope, sized it up and tied it securely to the wooden seat he made in his shed.

REVEREND MATTHEWS. His name jumped out at me even before I reached the gate. I stretched out my hand to ring the bell and four huge dogs ran out to the gate, barking and creating a fuss. The gardener, a tall man with a big stick and a machete came up to the gate, calling the dogs by name and telling them to be quiet. I told him I had come to see the Reverend. The man let me in. "Come in, Miss. De dogs calm down once yuh in de yard." I followed him towards the verandah and waited.

A lady in a white cap and apron came out. Did I want a glass of lemonade? The Reverend would be a few minutes because he was with someone. I was thirsty. The gardener went back to tend the plants and grass. Two of the four dogs sat in front of me and watched my every move. They didn't bark, they just sat looking at me.

"Deh won't bite," said the lady. "Dem only want to get used to yuh smell." I tried not to look into their eyes and pretended that I wasn't scared. The house and yard were big. From the outside it didn't seem that big because of the many trees that blocked it from the street. My mouth watered when a ripe East Indian mango fell to the ground. There were more down there, unattended, uneaten. Each time I moved my feet the dogs looked up and growled. Time passed and I rehearsed my speech to the Reverend. The gardener was busy raking leaves and the dogs were still looking at me.

Finally he came out. A tall white-looking man with a balding head, he looked different outside of church. Thinner without the robes he wore at the service. He smiled at me. Maybe he wasn't as unapproachable as I had thought. He sat down next to me and asked, "Now, what can I do for you, miss?"

"Well sah, ah am a member of St. Luke's and so is mi mother, though she don't get to come out to church as often as she would like. Ah am in Miss Patterson confirmation class...and ah miss a few classes...but ah catch up on some lesson, and now ah hear from de teacher dat ah can't confirm."

"Well, those are the rules. We cannot allow you to confirm when you've missed a class. Every class is important. Each one teaches a different lesson. You will just have to wait until next year."

I wasn't getting through to him. Mama's face was right up on mine and the dress and the shoes and the shame. Feeling anxious and desperate, I tried again. "I know, sah, Reverend, but ah want to confirm very bad. Mi been doing some extra reading on mi own, and ah can get more lessons from yuh or de teacher and study dem hard."

"But you have to attend the classes. There is no point in you studying by yourself."

"Reverend," I said, almost in tears, "Ah did attend classes. Ah missed only a couple because my mother was very sick, we had no one to look after her. I am de only child she have and ah had to stay home and look after her. And ah come here all de way to talk to yuh, Reverend sir, because ah feel yuh, as a man of God, would understand," I sat back proudly, taking a sip of my lemonade and waiting for him to say yes, of course I could be confirmed.

"Well God will bless you, little miss, for looking after your sick mother, but you won't be in this confirmation class. I'm sorry."

"But sah," I attempted one last time, "my mother will die. She will get sicker, she has been looking forward to attending and seeing her one daughter confirm, sah. Dis is de best present ah could ever give to her in her sickness, sah." By now my tears were real even if my story was not.

The Reverend folded his whitish hands and sat quietly looking at me. It was hard to figure out whether he believed me. I was taking no chances though. I started a loud cry and talked more about my sick mother and what this disappointment would surely do to her health.

The gardener and the lady in the house looked like they believed the story, but all Reverend Matthews said was, "You go and tell her. She'll understand that we have to follow the rules of the church." Fresh tears came streaming down my face.

"Trust me," he said, gently taking my hand. "Trust me your mother will understand. If she doesn't and I can be of any help, tell her to ring me up."

I didn't bother to tell him that Mama didn't have a telephone, that no one on my street owned a telephone. I was too sad to say any of this. The Reverend looked at his watch and told me he had phone calls to make and more appointments that afternoon.

The Reverend must be lying. If he knew Mama, if she were a personal friend of his, if she lived on this same street as he did, it would be easy for him to allow me to make up the lessons.

The gardener handed me a bag of ripe mangoes. I closed the gate behind me and took a mango out of the paper bag. I bit into it, not caring that it was unwashed. Not caring that Mama told me not to eat on the street. Not even caring who saw me eating on the street.

Tears rolling down my face, I bit even harder into the mango, its juices spilling all over my hands, running down to my elbows. I didn't care what people in the cars or the big houses thought.

Baked Goods

The cow at the top of the avenue was on the loose this morning, eating grass at the edge of Mr. Wong's property. The cow was on the loose and I had on a red blouse, my red pedal-pushers and Babes was wearing red shorts. We had never actually seen a cow running down anyone on our avenue, but it was an unspoken fact among us that cows on the loose, if provoked or in a bad temper, ran down and bucked people.

Half way up the road I handed Babes the cardboard box. I hated putting the box on my head, balancing it as I went down our avenue, turning on to Chisholm and then Waltham Park Road. The box was filled with patties, plantain tarts, gizzada and totoes which Mama baked once a week for the Chinese ice cream parlour at the foot of Waltham Park and Chisholm Avenue. My friend Babes came with me each Thursday evening, faithfully carrying the box on her head. I promised her dolls, comic books, a pair of guinea pigs, a trip to downtown Kingston with G and I. Anything. Sometimes the promises came true and when they didn't, I invented a story to explain why.

As we came closer to the cow, we walked on the far left side of the road. "Don't be scared of de cow," I assured Babes, though I was frightened myself. Crossing my index and middle fingers together, I prayed quickly and silently to God. Oh God, ah promise you anyting, just don't let de cow buck we. I do anyting God, go to Sunday school every Sunday, drop bad company, stop using cuss words. God, if yuh want I will even let Babes stop carrying de box on her head. God, show mi a sign, let de cow lef us alone and ah will do all of dose tings fi yuh. "Babes, just keep looking straight ahead," I said unsteadily, my knees beginning to shake. "Don't look at de cow, pretend 'im not dere."

The cow saw us coming, looked straight at us with its wide eyes and gave out the longest mo-o-o-o I ever heard from a cow, putting one foot forward to the left of the road. Frightened, we lost our balance, the box went flying off Babes head, scattering Mama's baked goods all over the road. Patties bruk-up in half, we quickly put them back in the box, brushing off the grass and dirt, and covered them with the foil paper Mama had packed around them.

We walked the rest of the way to the ice cream parlour, sober and solemn, with the box resting on my head. I asked God for one last chance, "Please don't let Mr. Wong notice de broken patties and cakes." With a final plea and without embarrassment, I said loudly, "God help me, please dis time, ah will prove to yuh dat ah can be a good girl."

"No, we can't take dis. What 'appen? It look like de box drop or someting. We can't pay fi dis. I tek de good ones and yuh tek back de bad ones to Lulu."

I waited quietly and patiently for Mr. Wong to count every last one of the battered cakes and patties and put them back in the box. Babes and I walked slowly toward home, I carrying the box, resentful and stony. I didn't know who to get upset at, Babes, God or Mr. Wong. I knew I'd have to tell Mama that I was the one who dropped the box—she didn't know that for months Babes had been carrying the box on her head to the shop. The way home stretched longer than ever. Feeling more rightful anger than sorrow, my thoughts were on how to tell Mama. Images of her sweating face over the hot oven didn't help matters. Poor Mama, if God had no pity on me, couldn't He have at least thought about Mama?.

As we were about to reach the turn onto my avenue, I said to Babes, "Come let we tek de short cut tru Mr. Wong yard." Mr. Wong's yard was wide and ran the entire avenue, starting from the top of the road and bordering on some of houses facing the right side of the street. His family lived on the first half of the land, surrounded by different varieties of mango trees. Further on there were ackee trees, breadfruit, plum, soursop and naiseberry trees. Part of the property was rented out to Mother Richard's Pocomania Church which congregated there ever Sunday in a large wooden structure they had built. Their building was marked by a high brick wall. It was common knowledge that people didn't cross Mr. Wong's yard as a short cut—he had a big sign saying PRIVATE PROPERTY - UNAUTHORIZED PERSONS AT RISK - BEWARE OF BAD DOGS. These were mostly for strangers, people living on the avenue knew that at certain times the dogs were locked away in their cages.

Babes agreed to come with me, though it was forbidden and if we were found out we would get licks. She also knew I was in a vex mood. We scaled the fence and walked through the yard, stopping only to pick mangoes. Eating and filling our pockets.

Surprising myself as much as Babes, I said, "Ah want to shit and ah not waiting till I get home. I going to shit right here, yuh wid me?"

Before she could respond, my pedal-pushers were halfway down my backside. Stooping, I pissed and shit right under the Bombay mango tree. I swore Babes to secrecy. We ran through Mr. Wong's grass, his mango orchard, past the church and barking dogs. The wind grabbed hold of my two stumpy pig tails all the way home.

Out de Candle

"**Out**de candle, out it. Granny a come." Muffled voices in unison as we blew out the candles that we had taken without permission from the kitchen drawer. In a flash the bedroom light was on, glaring at our closed eyes. We breathed heavily, in and out, our chests heaving up and down, as if we had been asleep all night.

Granny paused at our bedroom door before she turned off the light, satisfied that we were asleep and the sounds she heard might have come from the street.

Our bedroom was separated from hers by a single bathroom. Granny was Auntie Maggie's, Mama's and Aunt May's mother. Auntie Maggie and her husband, Uncle Blue, owned a tavern and spent a lot of time there. And Granny, who had moved from the country down to the city after her husband died, took complete charge of the household and total control of us on Saturdays.

Granny cooked and baked just like Mama, if not better. She said she was born with recipes in her head: plantain tarts, potato pudding, gizzadas baked to a crispness, with the right amount of granulated sugar sprinkled on top; home-made mango ice cream one week, soursop ice cream the next. The baking and variety seemed endless. Even when the baking stopped our nostrils were filled with the rich smell.

On Saturday evenings, after eating a full plate of dinner, we washed and dried dishes and pots. And finally our shower. Then we would sit on the verandah with granny. Saturday was Anancy story evening and Granny was the best storyteller we knew.

"Remember," she would say slowly, "Anancy is smart. Anancy walk on two leg. Remember Anancy is like human. Remember dat dere was a time when cat and rat were friends. Dog and cat best friends." Her slowness was ritual. We wanted her to get on with the story, but Granny did everything in her own time, so we kept quiet, impatient nonetheless.

"Once upon a time," she would finally begin, "Anancy de spider had a wife and three children. As yuh all know Anancy was a lazy man, luv to eat and sleep, his wife and children do all de work. One day 'im feeling good after 'im wife cook 'im a delicious breakfast of ackee and saltish and some ground provisions. So 'im seh to 'im wife. 'Wifey, how can ah help yuh?' Then he remember 'im mother-in-law. 'Ah know what wifey, what if ah go and help poor mother-in-law plant some corn? Poor ting working all alone.' 'Im wife happy and encourage 'im to go help her old mother. 'Im travel and travel, pass river, hill, grass, everyting. By de time 'im reach 'im hungry again and want to sleep. But de trickster 'im is, he put on a good face. 'Good morning, ma. Ah come to help yuh plant some corn.' De mother-in-law so grateful she tell 'im she going to cook 'im favourite dish of rice and peas, wid salt beef, onions, pepper, garlic and tomatoes. While she cooking Anancy working close by. After she finish cook, she cover up de pot and went on her way to help wid the planting of de corn."

Granny would pause, look around to see if she still had our attention. "Yuh know what de dutty Anancy do?" Any answer we gave was not quite the right one. She continued, her voice soft, slow, deliberate, then at other times quick.

"Before yuh know it, Anancy into de pot. 'Im tek off 'im hat and full it up wid de rich and peas. Den 'im start eat it fast, even though it a burn 'im tongue. Some people were passing by, and at de same time some hungry bird who smell de food descend on Anancy. 'Im want to hide de food because 'im hear 'im mother-in-law voice. In confusion 'im put de hatful of rice and peas on 'im head to hide it. 'Im head start burn. 'Im head start hurt 'im. 'Im wave 'im arm, 'im hop up and down, but de rice only seem to get hotter and hotter. Finally, 'im could tek it no longer, shame or no shame, so Anancy drag off de hat off 'im head and out fall de rice and peas, de salt beef, de onion, pepper and everyting else. Everybody start fe laugh."

Granny would pause again and look around. "Granny tell we what happen next nuh," Elithia would demand. Granny was in no hurry. She looked around at us again, this time smiling and stroking our heads. She began again in her own time.

"Well, Anancy was shame, but is he who bring it to 'imself, because of dishonesty, because of lies. So 'im so shame, wid all de people looking at 'im, and 'im mother-in-law shaking her head from side to side, dat 'im start talk to de grass. 'Hide me, hide me,' 'im beg de overgrown grass. Anancy dive in de grass hiding 'imself. And to dis day, Anancy hide in de grass. And to dis day 'im don't have no hair pon 'im head."

All too soon the stories would end and we would be made to put on our pyjamas and go to bed. Our protest of "just one more story, Granny," always fell flat. Granny treated us as if we were still in cloth diapers which meant bedtime was when the final shadow of the sun came down.

We were not allowed to watch television. "Only de devil's work," she tried to convince us. The Saturday night dances were sinful, and the radios played lyrics not fit to be heard by any good Christian.

After the Anancy stories it was prayer time. We knelt in front of Granny, eyes closed and recited the Twenty-third Psalm. Tossing and turning Saturday after Saturday, we thought of ways to outsmart Granny when she was asleep. It didn't take long. Several nights we snuck Uncle Blue's transistor radio in our room, listened to the hit parade and had our own dance contest. One night we had fallen asleep with the radio on. One of us must have rolled over on top of it, raising the volume. She shook us awake to the loud rock-steady beat that blared from the transistor. We were all quiet, trying to look innocent and confused by this strange object which had appeared in our bed. I pinched cousin Elithia under the covers a few times for, as usual, she was ready to give the whole story away and I wasn't sure whether Winnifred or I would be blamed. Granny carried on at length about us listening to vulgar music, about our young souls decaying, threatening to bring this to Auntie Maggie's attention the next morning. To our great relief she never did.

The telephone and the phone directory were our next diversion. "Peter Jackson" was a simple game, but it entertained us late into the night, our laughter bouncing back and forth in counterpoint to Granny's deep snores. "Hello," Winnifred would say in her put-on adult voice—she was into her fourteenth year—"may ah speak wid Peter Jackson?" There would be a pause from the other end and Winnifred would whisper to us, "I tink is 'im wife." Peter Jackson would come on the line. Now it would be someone else's turn to ask him, in the most serious of voices, "Mr. Jackson, did yuh order a pack of Peter Jackson cigarette?" We then hung up before he could respond.

Granny soon found out. We never knew how.

But no later were we found out than we devised yet another game to get us through boring, sleepless Saturday nights. We called this game "Out de Candle." Everything changed with this game: not only didn't we mind going to bed early, we began to look forward to it.

Each Saturday night one of us would be responsible for getting the candle and matches into our bedroom. Sometimes Granny would suspect that we were up to something and would wait us out and we would fall asleep. But we were young and energetic and we usually outlasted Granny.

We used the first part of the night to tell stories, sometimes about things that happened in our school yard after classes and other times new things about the "facts of life." We went to different schools, so there was always plenty to tell. Our conversations mostly would go like this: "Yuh ever see a bwoy's buddy?" Winnifred would start. I'd say, "Yes, of course, ah even see a man, when 'im was peeing." Winnifred would patiently wait for me to finish. "No, ah mean a bwoy ever willingly show yuh 'im buddy?" I had to admit not. "Yuh?" she turned to Elithia, more out of formality than interest. "Ah see dis bwoy who live down de road — all of it, even de balls."

With hands to her lips, she cautioned us. "Granny might wake up. 'Im like me very much, say he want to go steady wid me, and eventually engage me." Winnifred is laughing shyly. "He want to see my breast, so ah say show me your buddy first, and I'll show yuh my breast. He call me in de back of de yard, and take it all out and show me." She couldn't answer our questions fast enough. "Tell us how it look?" "Yuh get to feel it?" "How big?" "How long?" "Shuuuu" she cautioned again. "It long and mawga, like a pencil but de balls fat and round—yeah, I feel it, 'im let me."

I looked at her in awe. "So 'im touch yuh?" I ran ahead. "No." I sucked my teeth and searched for her eyes in the darkness. "Yuh don't believe me?" she challenged. "Why should ah let any little bwoy touch me up, what if ah get pregnant?"

When Granny's snores were coming through strong and loud and steady, we would start on part two of "Out de candle." The most dangerous half.

Our thin, rakey bodies were beginning to take on shape, waists beginning to look different from our hips, breast sharp and pointed, hair growing at an alarming rate in our underarms and between our legs. We were fascinated by this hair. Would it know when to stop? Who had the most hair? Did we all have the same colour and texture? Candle lit, two of us would hold it over the third's naked body and explore our growing breasts, our hips curving ever so subtly, the tiny hairs sprouting up between our legs and underarms like new grass. Sometimes our muffled giggles would ring through our room, past the bathroom and into Granny's room. Those times, we would wait quietly, expecting Granny. When she passed through the room we would pretend sleep, the candle and matches safely concealed.

It was on one such Saturday night, that Granny finally claimed victory. We had managed to fool her several nights, blowing out the candles just seconds before she entered our rooms. This night we were laughing louder than ever, bold in our new game and our ability to outsmart her. Whenever she came in the room and turned the lights on, we would be feigning sleep, masks of innocence on our faces. The lights would go out. We would wait for the snores. The candle would be re-lit. That night it was my turn to lie naked. I thought I saw a shadow through our half closed door, but I paid no attention, revelling in Elithia's envy over the progress of my breasts and hair between my legs. Then the door opened swiftly just as a piece of hot candle wax fell onto the corner of my leg. I smelt my own hair burning. I heard Winnifred and Elithia's laughter.

The lights went on. Granny standing a ways off, looking. Me stone stark naked. Winnifred with candle in hand bending over me, and Elithia pulling on my breast to feel the hardness.

"Good God, look at de wickedness going on under thy roof!" I was cold. The candle was still flickering in the light. "Jesus, God. Put on yuh clothes yuh serpent," she pointed at me with her cane. And yuh two, OUT DE CANDLE!" "Jesus, Father, God, Lord," she spoke as if dictating into a tape recorder, "forgive dese sinners." She turned around as swiftly as she entered the room, leaving the light on. We waited. She did not return. We waited. There was no snore. Elithia fell asleep. Finally I turned off the light. With the moon hanging high above our window, I searched for Winnifred's face, afraid to speak. Her hands reached for mine in the blackness.

Crossroads

Peterkin Prep was my third school after Mama pulled me out of Congregational Hall Government School. I was ten years old and for a time trouble followed me everywhere. After the last fight in the school yard ended up in the street Mama decided to move me to a school where people paid to have their children attend.

The school was near Crossroads, in four rooms at the back of a huge colonial house with a big verandah and shiny wooden floors. We called our headmistress Ma Kin. She'd spent several years in England and had come back to Jamaica to start her own school. There were two other teachers besides Ma Kin. I remember them as kind people, but Ma Kin and I didn't hit it off, not that this hurt my popularity. Even when she caned me and said I was a good-for-nothing black girl, it seemed only to make me more popular.

I'd become especially tight with three girls, Marcia Maragh, an Indian girl, Anna Marie Lee, a Chinese girl, and Janet King, a light-skinned brown girl. We played jacks at lunch time and gossiped about all the other girls and sex and menstruation. None of us had gotten our period and the most any of us had ever done was to kiss a boy on the cheek, but that didn't stop us from going on at great length.

One day during English class a girl was reciting a Longfellow poem and I was bored. Earlier that day I had scraped my knee on the fence in the back and though I had washed off the blood, my knee was still bleeding. I took out a piece of tissue paper, and wiped my knee, rolled up the paper and put it in the bend of my elbow. "What's dis?" I whispered to Anna Marie.

Anna Marie giggled, nudged Marcia who nudged Janet. Before I knew it Ma Kin was upon me, forcing me to stand up on my desk holding my left ear with my right hand and my left hand holding my right foot. I had to explain to the entire class what I meant by the Kleenex tissue with blood in the bend of my elbow. The class shrieked with laughter as I tried to keep my balance. I kept my eyes open as to who laughed the loudest. Ma Kin kept me after school for an hour to write over and over that I would never do this again, but at least I'd escaped the cane. It was still light outside when Ma Kin dismissed me with a warning that I could be expelled for corrupting the minds of the other students.

I took the short cut to Crossroads through the back of St. Luke's Church and walked through the gully, buying a snowcone on the way. I sat in the churchyard for a while, wondering how I always ended up being the one caught. Marcia found me there. "Did she beat yuh? Did she send a letter home to yuh mother? What she say to yuh?"

That evening we decided to form a club. We'd meet in the open land across from the Tom Redcomb Library. Our club would be called The Four O'Clock Club, I would be president and Marcia would be vice-president. We'd ask girls to join and then there would be an initiation. Monday the message passed around the school, with the meeting place set for the open land across from the library. Marcia and I were the first to arrive and Janet was next. Anna Marie couldn't come because her parents sent a driver to collect her after school each evening. Some mornings on the crowded bus to school I wondered what it would be like to be chauffeur driven to school, but by evening when the school bell rang to let us out, I'd be thinking of snowcones and romping with Marcia behind St. Lukes.

The open land was full of fruit trees and while we waited on the others, we ate our bellies full of plums, mangoes and whatever was in season. After sucking the last drop of juice from my mango I threw the seed at Marcia. As the other girls started to come in, we jumped up, almost knocking each other down, as if the same idea came to the two of us at the same time. Seven girls had come. We waved to them excitedly and sat them down to talk about the club, making up the rules as we went along. Marcia started off.

"Now none of dis must get back to Ma Kin or any of de other girls in de school. We are all blood sisters and de first ting to do is rub our blood together. So each girl have to prick her big finger wid dis pin and we will all rub our blood together." Marcia produced a big safety pin from her bag, and pricked her finger. A few of the girls flinched, but all put out their thumbs. As Marcia pricked each finger, the more queasy ones looked away. Then it was my turn.

"O.K. De next ting is dat anybody who have any stories about sex or period have to talk about dem. Anybody start her period or anybody kiss a bwoy, or ever see a adult only movie, or ever see a man or woman tings."

There were a lot of giggles and many voices talking excitedly.

"One at a time, one at a time!" I shouted. "We are meeting once a week so we'll have plenty of time to hear everybody's story."

I shot a look at Janet, who sat quietly, and introduced her as the secretary of the club. "Now Janet will take up de dues, which will be a penny a week."

There was a squirm and I continued quickly, "Dat is to buy snowcone and anyting else we want."

"And one more ting," Marcia said. "We have any fight among us, we settle it. We bring it here, not to Ma Kin. We is our own judge."

"But how we going to settle it?" asked one of the girls. "Never mind about dat now," said Marcia. "We will settle it when de time comes."

I stayed out of trouble for a long time because the club was where we settled fights. We talked about boys and adult-only movies, things we'd read in the newspapers about men sexing women and each other.

When jimbling was in season I climbed the tree and shook it so hard a wasp stung me on the eyebrow, swelling it all up. Mama sent me off to school the next day, saying it was my own fault. Ma Kin, fass as ever, demanded to know what happened. I told her I'd been stung in my back yard, a test to see if anybody would talk, but no one did.

We met as usual that week and the next. The swelling had gone down considerably, but I stayed far away from that tree. Instead we forced Jennifer to climb for jimbling. She did and surprised us by not getting stung. We ate jimbling and as Marcia and I wandered around the open land we came across some white, plastic balloon-like things. Fascinated, we took them up and looked for more. We tried to figure out what they were, but nobody really knew, so we made it our mission to find out by next week. At home I rushed through feeding the fowls and guinea pigs and after getting Mama's newspaper for her, I pulled Joy aside.

"Joy, guess what? We see this ting like a balloon, lots in de open land."

Joy sniggered, then broke into whoops and gasps. "Dat's not a balloon, gal. Dat is a condom."

"A what?"

Joy whooped again, grabbed her sides and tumbled onto a chair. "Men wear it when dem having sex so dat de woman don't get pregnant."

"Are yuh sure? Ah don't want to be giving false information, yuh know." I wanted to be first with the news.

The next afternoon we went off to the open land. Holding the condom in front of her, Marcia asked the circle if anybody knew what it was. "A balloon. Anybody can see dat," announced Jennifer to a chorus of um-hms. Marcia sucked her teeth.

"No, no," I jumped in. "Man use it so woman don't get pregnant."

"Yuh lie, gal! No such ting!" scoffed Janet.

Marcia settled it. "She right. And it also fi disease, to mek sure de man don't get any disease from de woman." Later I asked Marcia how she knew about disease. "My mother's boarder Monty, tell me all about it."

We spent the rest of the meeting carefully examining it, using a stick to demonstrate.

"What if it burst?" Janet asked.

"Yuh don't see how tick it is? How could it burst?" But I filed the question away to ask Joy.

Marcia and I counted out money from the dues and sent Janet and Aileen to buy snowcones, keeping the change for ourselves as vice-president and president.

At school the next morning Ma King called Marcia and me to her private room. She knew all about the club. Calling me "nega" and Marcia "coolie gal," Ma Kin accused us of "leading good pickney astray." If we complained about these slurs to our parents, we'd get the beatings of our lives, so we had to keep the insult to ourselves. Ma Kin sent us home with a note suspending us for a week. As we left the grounds the other girls were quick with sympathy, but we couldn't get a word out of anybody about who told on us. Marcia and I walked through the gully, then through St. Luke's Church and rested on the church steps to figure out our next move.

Marcia was definite. "Well, mi know one ting. Ah not takin' dis home because dat is de end of me."

I sat quietly, still in shock. "So what we going to do?"

"Well, we just won't show de letter and we'll pretend we going to school. Meet mi at Crossroads tomorrow morning just like we going to school."

Marcia and I spent the next morning walking in Woolworth's. After various adults inquired why we weren't in school, we bought lunch and went off to the open land.

We talked about many things, our favourite topic being about sex. Marcia said sometimes she put a pillow between her legs and it felt good. I confessed I laid on top of my pillow. We always ended by talking about Ma Kin.

"Yes. Is just because we don't have chauffeur picking us up, and because mi not a light skin girl or better still, Chinese.

"Yes," said Marcia. "And because we didn't come straight from another prep school and she have no right calling me 'coolie gal.'"

"I wonder if Anna Marie have anyting to do with dis?"

"But she wasn't dere. It would have to be someone dere who tell her."

We waited until late to see if the girls would show up, but no one came to the open land. The next day we waited again and no one came.

The third day we decided to go off to Hope Gardens and packed street dresses in our school bags so we could change out of our school uniforms in Woolworth's washroom. We wandered around Hope Gardens, the zoo, went through the maize several times and watched lovers together.

We were back in school on Monday, looking sombre and not talking. We didn't want Ma Kin to be suspicious about whether we'd been beaten by our parents. At lunch time Marcia and I sat at separate ends of the yard, reading our school books and not talking to anyone. By Wednesday we were sure we'd convinced Ma Kin that we had changed our ways. Whenever one of the girls would ask if we were going to meet again we'd shrug that we didn't know what they were talking about.

By the middle of the next week I braved myself to pass a note to Janet, asking if she knew who'd told. She wrote back that she would tell us all at Crossroads. Marcia and I left separately and met at St. Luke's Church to walk over to the open land.

Janet was waiting for us and she had the whole story. "De weak link is Aileen. Anna Marie promise her ride in chauffeur car and Aileen tell Anna Marie everyting." Janet said the rest of the girls would back us. "After all, is de club settle fight."

I had a plan. "But we have to be careful. So close to de end of school term, we don't want dis on our report card."

It couldn't have been a better last day of school. I won the sponge cake raffle with ticket number fifty-five. I shared out the cake with a big slice for Ma Kin.

Anna Marie handed Ma Kin the note Marcia had written saying that Anna Marie was taking the bus home today as a treat for the last day of school. We went running over St. Luke's hill, picking flowers, putting them in our hair and singing.

At last we were at the open land. Jennifer climbed the jimbling tree while the rest of us sat eating mangoes. I wiped my hands on my legs and turned to Anna Marie "Who tell pon us?"

Surprised, Anna Marie looked at Aileen. Aileen looked down. Marcia beckoned Janet to bring her mango seed. Janet placed it in Anna Marie's hand.

"Come, come," I said to them. "Is between de two a yuh. Settle it. Unno both to blame fi unno big mout.'

We made a circle around them, cheering and shouting.

Marcia hit the mango into Anna Marie's face who leapt upon Aileen, using her fingernails to draw blood from her face. Then Aileen grabbed on to Anna Marie's long hair. We cheered. The sun was disappearing and we had to get home, but summer holidays would start tomorrow.

Cornmeal
Porridge

S ome mornings the porridge was lumpy and we still had to
drink it all. We tried feeding it to the dogs, but Mama would
be outside, sitting under the blackie mango tree, watching.

That's what I remember most about the summer holidays I spent
at my grandmother's house. I called my father's mother, "Mama." I
also called my own mother, "Mama." Cousin Molly lived with our
grandmother, along with Auntie Babsie—Cousin Molly's mother,
Uncle Freddy and Auntie Pam and, of course, Papa, grandmother's
husband.

My grandmother's house wasn't at all like Mama's house. She
had a small two-bedroom house with a tiny living room, a dining
room that became another bedroom at night and a small verandah
with red tiles, looking out on the street. At the back of the yard was
my grandmother's one-room kitchen and attached to it was the shower room and separated by another wall was our toilet. A cistern where
we washed our faces, dishes and clothes was around the corner.

I liked my grandmother's little house. I liked the sense of family
spilling over from the photo albums into the tiny rooms. Some faces

were familiar, others lived far away in Canada, England and the United States. Sometimes there wouldn't be enough room to sleep, but there was always room for music and laughter.

I slept in the dining room in a double iron bed with Auntie Pam and Uncle Freddy. Cousin Molly slept with her mother in one of the bedrooms and my grandparents slept in the other.

My father's mother was a light-skinned woman with long, straight, pitch-black hair stretching down to the middle of her back. My Cousin Molly and I loved to brush my grandmother's hair and ask her about her younger days. We never tired of this or of listening to her stories about her white father, a German landowner in Westmoreland, and her half-Indian mother.

Sometimes it seemed as if all we talked about was long hair, white blood stirred up with African blood and straight noses. Mama was never mentioned in these discussions. She had strong African features. I was the same colouring as my mother but with some of my father's features, so I managed to escape some of the ridicule about skin colour and African features, especially the lips and nose.

Our grandmother always sided with us when Papa was harsh. He would sometimes demand we sweep the yard three times a day, or forbid us to watch anything except the news on television or complain about the music on the radio being too loud and vulgar. But her support was always silent.

There was only one place where she didn't side with us and that was the corn meal porridge. She would say. "Not one drop I want to see out here in de dog plate." And we would have to eat it, lumps and all.

Every morning she cooked corn meal porridge which we ate with hard-dough bread. Some mornings the porridge was good, piping hot, sweetened with Betty Condensed Milk, vanilla and nutmeg. On the lumpless days, we would clean out the enamel dish with our tongues and fingers, often begging for more.

Freddy and Pam, our aunt and uncle, were five and six years older than us and more like older cousins than aunts and uncles. When I spent summer holidays at my grandmother's I went to her

Methodist church on Lyndhurst Road. We left the house every Sunday with Freddy and Pam. They hated the idea of Sunday school and for our silence gave us threepence each not to tell Mama and Papa that they did not go. We didn't know what they did when we left them, but we were content with our threepence.

My grandparents' house reminded me of my friend Jackie's, with its strictness and rules, especially when Papa was around. The locked gate was opened only for us to go to the shop for my grandmother and to church and school. We were allowed to play only with the girl next door. Her name was Deanne and my grandmother was friends with her mother, Mrs. Morris. We didn't particularly like Deanne, and if we had had the freedom to choose our playmates, she would have been last on our list. We might not have been her first choice of friends either, but any companion was better than none.

Deanne was a plump, round-faced girl with skin the colour of dark fudge. Her lips were a rosy pink, making her look like she had lipstick on. Her hair, ironed every Saturday by her mother, was pressed back from her face and held tightly by an elastic band. She wore a pair of gold sleeper earrings that in the light seemed to steal a piece of the sun. I can't remember exactly what it was about her that we didn't like. Perhaps it was her boastful nature, her self-assuredness, so much like an adult's. Perhaps it was because she was never forced to eat corn meal porridge. She seemed to be always eating ice cream and candies and she had an endless supply of bubble gum.

When she came over to our house we played baseball, hopscotch, dandy-shandy or jacks. She was a good player and most always won. Deanne had some magical power in games, especially jacks. I would demand a re-match only to be humiliated by her winning again. We weren't graceful losers, but neither was she a gracious winner.

Cousin Molly held her anger better than I did. Always there to caution me about the licks we would receive from our grandmother if I punched Deanne, many times Molly held me back from sending Deanne a blow in her plump stomach with my fists.

On one of those days that we absolutely hated Deanne we overheard Miss Grant talking about her. It was morning and there were more lumps than ever in our corn meal porridge. Our grandmother sat conspicuously under the mango tree outside the dining room, waiting for us to clean our bowls. But the lumps were so big and grainy that our throats tightened at every spoonful.

The sun was heating up and the room was heavy without even a little breeze coming in. We sat at the dining table with its plastic table cloth, the wooden window wide open. It was getting close to lunch time and our breakfast remained on the table, still lumpy and now cold, the flies freely pitching over our faces and into our bowls. Our grandmother called in to us, "Eat de porridge. If unnu tink unnu putting one foot outside today, unnu making a big mistake, not widout all dat porridge eaten."

Mama then went on to compare Deanne with us, loud enough for the neighbours on both sides to hear. Through the dining room window we saw Deanne dancing behind the wire fence, her tongue sticking out at us, her lips pinker than ever and her gold earring glistening in the sun.

Pam and Freddy had left the house early, managing somehow to escape the wretched corn meal porridge. Mama claimed that we were growing bodies and needed the corn meal porridge much more than they did.

It was while we sat staring at the porridge that we overheard the story about Deanne. Mama was at the cistern pipe, catching water for the dishes, and above the running water we heard Miss Grant from next door calling to Mama.

"Howdy, Miss Thorne. How yuh doing today? It look like dose two girls giving yuh a hard time today?" she inquired nosily.

"Yes, tink dem is big 'oman, tink dey too big for corn meal porridge. Don't know what dis younger generation coming to."

"Is so dem stay," added Miss Grant. She continued, "Miss Thorne, yuh don't know what a just hear not too long, dat Miss Morris and her husband adopt Deanne, dat Deanne not dem own."

We crept from around the dining table and moved closer to the window to get a good view of our grandmother and Miss Grant. Miss Grant's eyes were wide open, waiting for a shocked response from our grandmother.

"Where yuh hear dat from?" our grandmother asked.

"From across de street dis morning."

"Well ah guess Deanne belong to dem now. If dem adopt her, dat mean dem is her rightful mother and father," our grandmother said, putting an end to the conversation.

Miss Grant's face fell in like a just-burst balloon, but she didn't try to continue the discussion. It was hard for us to tell from our grandmother's face or tone whether this was news to her or whether Miss Morris had confided in her. She turned around unexpectedly and her eyes made six with ours as we rushed back to the porridge.

"Hold it right dere," she said.

She came close to the window, her face hard, and between closed teeth she said, "If ah ever hear one word out of yuh two 'bout dis, de police will have to come and tek me out of dis yard."

We knew our grandmother's threats were not to be taken lightly, but we'd never met an adopted girl before and we were made wild with excitement by this news about Deanne.

In no time our grandmother was back in position under the mango tree. Like a thunderclap, her loud voice came through the window to remind us that we still had the corn meal porridge to finish.

"Look, ah not joking with unnu, is now past midday and unnu don't finish de porridge. If unnu tink unnu going to get away, yuh better change dat story because unnu going to sit dere all night with de porridge until Papa come home."

That was not what we wanted to hear. Our grandmother's threats were serious, but they could not be compared to what Papa might do.

Now Deanne was hooked onto the wire fence, her tongue darting up and down, her big round face snarled up. She went inside her mother's kitchen and came out with a big ripe mango in her hand. She danced with the mango, then bit into it.

"Ah getting tired of sitting here. Look at Deanne. She finish her breakfast and lunch long time, and unnu still eating."

What Molly then did was so sudden that I almost missed seeing it. She closed her eyes and in three quick swallows gulped down the remainder of her cold, fly-ridden porridge. I pleaded with Molly to do the same for me. She pretended not to understand.

"Mi wi do anyting Molly, anyting in return," I whispered desperately. "Sweep de yard every morning, your side and my side. Clean out de toilet, wash dishes, anyting." Molly didn't answer, and with a pained look on her face, she got up quickly from the table.

Molly's exit from the table started our grandmother going again.

"Amen, good fi yuh Molly." She turned on me now. "A 'oman yuh is? When yuh going to finish? How yuh so stubborn, gal?" She reached into her purse and sent Molly to the meat shop. On her way out the gate Molly and I eyed each other. She motioned for me to follow her example.

Deanne was singing some nonsense song, pitching her voice high over the fence. I was in a fury from head to toe. I wanted to wring her neck.

I measured the porridge in the enamel bowl and realized I had at least nine spoonfuls left. How to get rid of it? I thought of throwing it in the flower bowl on top of the fridge, but our grandmother knew that trick. I thought of putting it down my underwear, but she would notice the wetness and I would probably have to stay in wet lumpy underwear as punishment. I tried to gulp it down the way Molly did, but it stuck in my throat. My eyes tightly closed, I could feel the big round lumps. I was sure I would vomit, but I didn't. Our grandmother was triumphant as I showed her the empty dish.

When Molly came back from the shop we complained to each other about our morning ordeal—it was all Deanne's fault—and plotted about how we would survive the rest of these summer holiday mornings.

Evening came quickly, and Deanne was over the fence as usual, asking our grandmother if she could come play jacks with us. That evening we didn't feel much like playing with Deanne, but she was right there and we couldn't say anything. We tried to tell our grandmother with our eyes that we wanted nothing to do with Deanne, at least not that day, but our grandmother ignored us.

We grudgingly played with her. As usual, she was winning all the way. Finally I could take it no longer. "Deanne," I said, "How come yuh so dark like burn fudge and Mr. and Mrs. Morris so brown?"

She laughed in that self-assured way we hated and continued to play the jacks.

"Yuh not answering?" I pestered.

She paused with the ball, her hands up in the air, and in a voice that sounded older than our eight years, she replied, "It never boddered me, so ah never wonder about it. Dere is a lot of families like dat around."

She continued to win and there was nothing we could do to change her luck. It was not something I decided to do and I don't know why I did it, except she was winning and she was such a show-off about it and her gold earring looked so perfect in her ears that I snapped at her, "Deanne, yuh ever really wonder why yuh so dark and your mother and father so light?"

She looked at me with maddening patience and just kept on playing the jacks. I nudged Molly to continue. "Yes, Deanne. Just look how dey light. Yuh ever ask dem anything about dat?"

Deanne grabbed up her jacks off the verandah tile and made her way to the gate.

"Go wey adopted gal, yuh gwan like yuh nice. Adopted gal, adopted gal, adopted gal!" I taunted.

She stood at the gate frozen and shocked.

"Yuh lie. Yuh lie! Yuh are a dirty liar!" She shouted back, forgetting her grownup ways. I looked at Molly to say something.

"Den go and ask yuh mother, Miss Morris. See if we a lie. Mek her tell yuh dat yuh adopted."

Deanne's face looked like a pail of water had been thrown on it. She rushed out of the yard in tears. We sat on the tiles of the verandah and laughed, drunk with wickedness. We had made Deanne pay for this morning. At last we'd made her cry and act her age. We no longer heard her crying. We didn't hear her mother's voice across the fence, telling our grandmother what had happened. Nor did we hear our grandmother coming around the bend with Papa's belt in her hand.

The heavy leather strap slapped down on our backs, across our faces, on our bottoms, across our bellies, on our feet. I remember screaming and then our grandmother's face behind the smelling salts. "Unnu go to bed now. No dinner fi unnu."

I was so tired from running and from the licks that when I fell asleep I was sure I would never wake up again. That night I dreamt of corn meal porridge, corn meal pudding, corn bread, corn meal wrapped in banana leaf, dukuno.

Gem

We'd both failed the common entrance exam the first time we sat for it and this was our last chance for a scholarship to high school. The first time Jackie was sure she'd passed. We'd waited eagerly for the morning newspapers to see the results, scanning the columns of names, but ours weren't there.

There was a lot of talk from our parents about the exams being fixed, about quotas, about examiners being paid off by well-to-do families. Jackie's mother told Mama that it had been going on for years and that we'd probably passed but were bounced off to fit in some monied students. Every so often she would pause, sigh and say, "But wha fi do?"

We had one more chance to sit for the exam, and Mama, upon the advice of one of the customers who frequented Auntie Maggie's bar, decided to change my school once again. This new one, I was told, was a very proper preparatory school where the fees were high but I was sure to get a scholarship. The customer, who recommended it said the examiners also favoured certain schools in giving out the scholarships and this was one such school.

The summer before school started I was in a constant state of excitement. I told everyone on the avenue about going to this new preparatory school. Mama cautioned me several times to be still; "Yuh talk too much, it nuh good to tell so much people about yuh business." She was sitting at the Singer sewing machine, putting the last touches on my new school uniform, and I was sitting on the floor of the bedroom we shared, polishing my brown loafers. Mama warned me, "Just behave yuhself and no more fighting. Dat kind of behaviour finish. Leave dat behind now. Is decent children at dis school. Hooligans not at dis school."

The next week I took the bus uptown to my new school. As I went through the gate my heart raced. This school was smaller than my others: set in a large paved yard with an immense flowering tree was one large room with high wooden windows that opened wide. A large house sat away from the one-room school, both owned by the headmistress, a white Englishwoman who had come to live in Jamaica a long time ago.

I was early, the first one there. I walked into the yard uncertainly and sat at the first bench I reached. Soon several cars drove by, dropping off other girls and boys. Quite a few were Chinese, like Anna Marie, a girl at one of my other schools. Some white girls and a few blacks with very light skins piled out of cars and took benches. As we waited for the teacher we sat looking at each other from head to toe. A bell rang, pulling us upright on the benches as a neatly-dressed woman marched through the gate and introduced herself as Mrs. Martin, our teacher. She had a kind face and smooth chocolate-brown skin. We stood up as she called out our names and that gave us another chance to check on one another.

"...Marlene Budwiser, Gem Jennison, Marcia Johnson, Paul Martin, Junior Rockford..." Mrs. Martin's voice bellowed. I had turned my attention to Gem Jennison and almost missed the calling of my name. Gem's smile lit up her face, but it was her eyes that caught me, large, deep brown and dancing. I knew at once that I wanted to be her best friend.

The morning passed quickly. Soon it was time for lunch and Mrs.

Martin directed us to a large open area, with a covering in case of rain. Gem had already taken out her lunch and was eating. I went over and sat near her. She smiled and I greeted her shyly. Marlene, a white girl, came over and sat next to Gem. She introduced herself but ignored me as she went on at length to talk about herself. Gem said she came from the Cayman Islands and I jumped into the conversation and asked her what it was like.

"Dem have coconut trees? Is it different from Jamaica?"

Before Gem could answer, Marlene leapt at me like a wild goat. "Why do you ask such ignorant questions? Why don't you just keep your mouth shut. People like you shouldn't be let into this kind of school."

I charged right back at her that I paid the same fee and that I was free to go any place I wanted, that she couldn't talk to me like that. I didn't realize I was shouting until I saw the crowd around us and Mrs. Martin making her way towards us. I was sure that I would be punished, maybe even expelled. I was surprised that Mrs. Martin did not punish me. It was the white girl who had to apologize to me.

After that day Marlene and Gem and I became inseparable. Later Marcia, Mrs. Martin's niece, became part of our group. The four of us did everything together: we sat beside each other in class, ate lunch together and we left school together most days. Some evenings we would all walk over to Marcia's house. It had big mango trees, plum trees, and a jackfruit tree. She had two maids, a gardener and a brand new bicycle! I'd never owned one and didn't even know how to ride. Neither did Gem and we had fun learning, even though we fell off several times. After our bike rides we would climb in the tree house with the bread and jam, cookies and milk that one of the maids fixed for us and tell stories.

We didn't talk a lot about scholarships and future plans. We seemed to spend more time riding bicycles, eating bread and jam and gossiping about other students. But I liked my new school very much and admired Mrs. Martin who, unlike Ma Kin and her shouts of "nega" and "black gal," encouraged me in my writing and math. And I was sure that when I sat for the common entrance I would get a scholarship.

When we didn't go to Marcia's house we would go to Marlene's or sometimes Gem's. It was at Marlene's house that I first tasted peanut butter. Like most people on my avenue, Mama didn't go to supermarkets but to grocery shops and the market.

Marlene's house was big, like Marcia's, but cold. Maybe it was that it had tiled floors where Marcia's house had wooden floors. Marlene had more fruit trees than I'd ever seen in any of the yards in my neighbourhood. Pomegranate, cherry, pineapples and others whose fruit I'd only ever seen in the market.

Sometimes when we were up in Marcia's tree house Marlene and Marcia would talk about their parents. Once Marlene boasted about not having anything to do but her homework when she got home. She snickered when I asked if she didn't have to wash her own socks and underwear. "Our maid does that," she smugly replied.

Marlene wanted to go on and on, but Marcia cut her off when she probed about how things were done at Marcia's house. "No. Millie does that, but sometimes I do too."

Gem said she didn't have a helper and washed her own. I glared at Marlene with satisfaction, but this didn't stop Marlene and she went on to talk about her big house and big television and her big everything that was always bigger than everyone else's.

They never came to my house. And though I had a lot of things they didn't have, like guinea pigs, chickens and fowls, I took it for granted that they all lived in big houses uptown and I lived downtown and they wouldn't be interested in visiting me.

Marlene teased Gem constantly about Junior Rockford, who liked Gem and followed her around like a lost dog. To the rest of us he was just another short, obnoxious boy who boasted constantly about how he would someday inherit his father's car company. Gem didn't seem to care too much for him, but she treated him kindly. Sometimes Junior would even walk with us to Marcia's house, then turn around and leave, provoking us to shouts of "Mrs. Rockford! Mrs. Rockford!" Gem would never curse back, never look hurt, never look pleased. She made it so easy for us to tease her. I admired and loved her so.

One Saturday I invited Gem to my house. I wanted to be with her alone and for her to see my guinea pigs, the room I shared with Mama and my secret place under the house. I liked Marlene and Marcia, but I wasn't sure they would like it at my house. I thought they would be bored.

Gem promised to come at two in the afternoon. I was up by eight o'clock, wiping and polishing the verandah, cleaning out the house bottom, scrubbing the guinea pig pen and leaving them fresh grass. I made lemonade with brown sugar and Mama baked a sponge cake. At two I looked up the avenue and saw her coming. She was so beautiful, with a red bow holding her thick black hair together. She wore a red and white dress with flower designs all over and white socks and black shoes. I proudly introduced her to Mama and then took her to the room we shared. Gem had brought house clothes with her to change into. I told her where the bathroom was, but Gem said she could change her clothes right there. I admired her confidence. She already had breasts and she wasn't self-conscious at all. She also had white panties on. I sat admiring the way she wore white —everything I had white had turned grey. We had never talked about breasts and the hairs that were growing in strange places on our bodies and I wanted to see what her breasts looked like under her white bra, but I just sat, saying nothing, afraid she'd run away.

We went out shortly after to the guinea pig pen. Gem spent a long time looking at the guinea pigs and talking to them. She wanted to take a pair home with her, but Mama insisted that she ask her mother first. I didn't introduce Gem to any of my friends on the avenue. I wanted to keep her to myself. So when Jackie and then Joy and Tony came and banged on the gate, I went out and told them we were busy talking important things they wouldn't understand.

Gem was eager to see my marbles, my dolls, and my dolls' furniture that G had built. We crept into the coolness of the house bottom. We sat on the ground, the chill of the earth against our legs. I showed her how to make mud cakes with dirt and a bit of water and how to get the cake to hold by putting it in a match box for a few minutes. We set the doll's table and put the mud cake on it and Gem arranged the dolls around the table while I tided up the dolls' bed.

I could see that Gem was having fun and that she liked playing house and making mud cakes. She said she didn't have a house bottom, but she did have lots of dolls and played house by herself. We talked about all kinds of things, coming from under the house bottom only to drink lemonade and eat Mama's sponge cake. Back under the house bottom, I asked her about the Cayman Islands and she told me about her father who still lived in Cayman and had remarried. I told Gem about my father and his barbershop, my Auntie Maggie, my Cousin Molly and the others in my family and helping my Auntie May who owned a grocery store. It was easy talking to Gem. She was so different from Marlene and Marcia. I took my treasure box with its store of snapshots of my friends and family and cut-outs from magazines from its hiding place in the house bottom. There were scraps of houses, people, flowers, things I might see sometime if I ever visited Canada or any other far-off place. I even had a cut-out of snow on a mountain.

Gem grew quiet but I could feel her warm breath on my neck. I turned to see if she was still looking at the scrapbook. She was staring intently at my pictures and had that smile I'd liked so much that first day at school. I couldn't help it, I kissed her on the mouth. She leaned over and kissed my eyes, my plaits and my mouth. We sat for what seemed like a long time, leafing through snapshots and cut-outs we'd already seen. It felt so perfect. The dolls around the table eating mud pies, their beds close by, my marbles, the photos, Gem beside me in my favourite place. I burst out, "Gem mi love yuh."

"Yes," said Gem, taking my hand. "We're best friends."

A banging at the gate interrupted us. I was sure it was Joy or Tony, impatient for a peep at Gem, for I had told them how beautiful she was. When I crawled from under the house bottom and stomped off towards the gate, I knew exactly what I would tell them. "Go to hell and leave mi."

I marched to the gate, with Gem trailing behind me. At first all I could tell was that it wasn't anybody from my avenue. But as I reached the gate, the figure became more familiar. It was Junior Rockford.

"What yuh want? Yuh cyaan see we busy?"

"Don't be like that," Gem implored me. "And anyway, I have to be getting home, it's almost dinner time."

I wouldn't let Junior through the gate, but Gem left soon after, promising she'd see me on Monday.

I never figured out how Junior Rockford found out where I lived and it was a long time before I felt like going back under the house bottom.

Jack-the-Painter

As far back as I can remember, Jack-the-Painter came once a year to paint the inside of our house. The tips of his brush would flick into the corners of the wall and then on to larger areas, boldly striking the old colours. I watched his stubby fingers for hours as he stroked away, the blue, the pinks, mixing two colours together and turning them into another. I especially liked the pink watermelon colour he mixed to use on the living room wall and the trimming in white.

Jack was a short, thick, black man. Mama had known him for years. High on his ladder, I watched him for days, first painting the verandah, then the living room, the kitchen, the hallways and finally the bedroom and the bathroom. Jack started early in the morning before I woke up and ended in the evening when the first shadows came down. Mama cooked a lot while Jack was around, feeding him every evening. Most days the smell of fried chicken or a pot of tripe competed with fresh paint and turpentine.

In awe of Jack-the-Painter, I decided that when I grew up I wanted to be a painter just like him. Mama said only men painted, that she never knew of a woman painter, but that did not dissuade me. I told Jack about my plans and he agreed that painting was a good trade. He promised to teach me to paint. My first lesson took place one afternoon when the only area left to paint was our tiny bathroom. Jack sent me high on the ladder and he climbed up behind me. With the wall in front of me, he took my hand and, with his over mine, allowed me a few precious strokes. I felt so big and powerful up on the ladder, not at all like a child in pedal-pusher pants and loose cotton shirt covering a skinny frame.

The brush was still moving up and down, his hands still covering mine when I felt his left hand on my bottom. His stumpy fingers reached into my pedal-pushers and unbuttoned my pants, groping in my underneath. We continued to paint, up and down, up and down, the white wall turning a soft blue. I hated it. I wanted to tell him to stop, but I was afraid he wouldn't let me paint again. Jack's face at my back, he probed deeper in my underneath, his breathing thick like dust. I wanted to scream because it hurt.

All of a sudden I was afraid for Mama because if she found out, then Jack would be a dead man. I knew that much. I wanted to protect him and I wanted him to stop. It was close to Christmas and Mama was baking Christmas cakes and cooking food to freeze for the holidays. I could hear her singing *The Little Drummer Boy* in the kitchen and I knew she was happy. Jack didn't seem to care that Mama was so close. "Up and down," he kept saying, in a calm voice through his thick breathing. Finally he removed his hand.

"See how much yuh paint today," he said confidently. "It look nice. Yuh going to be a good painter."

I came off the ladder hating myself for keeping quiet, for still admiring his paint job, for being thankful that he let me hold his brush, for not telling Mama. Jack came into the kitchen with me and smiled at Mama, pieces of gold governing three of his teeth.

"Everything finish, Miss Lulu," he said. "Look how de house look new."

"Yes man, yuh really do a good job fi de money. Come and have some food."

Jack told Mama that he'd taught me to use a brush and that if I practised I could be a good painter someday. I sat and watched as he made much of Mama, her cooking and baking and her wonderful freshly-painted house. Mama served up more food. He ate my Mama's chicken, her rice and peas, salad, her potato pudding, ice cream and jello. Then Mama presented him with a home-baked black cake and a bottle of sorrel to take home to his family.

Months later I heard Jack-the-Painter had moved to England. The next year when it was close to Christmas another painter came. But I'd lost interest in becoming a painter. This time I didn't even watch the new painter paint.

Harbour View

Cock crowing, dog barking, breadfruit and ackee dropping from the trees, the voices of women from Mother Richard's church in the yard behind ours. Sunday mornings and Uncle Bunny.

Lazy Sunday mornings we would wake up to eat Mama's fried dumplings, plantains, ackee and boil banana. Sunday evenings it would be fried chicken, rice and peas cooked up with scallion and coconut milk and a salad of tomatoes and lettuce and freshly-made carrot juice to wash it down.

Sunday mornings. I remember the smell of hot-iron comb that I used to put through Mama's hair. Mama washed her hair every Sunday morning and when it was dry I would run the hot iron through her hair to straighten it. Uncle Bunny teasing Mama about the length of her hair and I pretending that I couldn't catch the ends to run the hot iron through them, and Mama, always good-natured, would join in our joke.

Uncle Bunny was a cook at Chin's Restaurant in downtown Kingston. He brought home Chinese food for us at night, served up with wonderful stories about his wealthy customers and how they dressed.

What I liked most about Sunday's was going off in the evenings with Uncle Bunny, his friend John and John's sister, Rose, to visit their other friends.

We always went to Harbour View, to the same big house with so many rooms and so much food and drink and music. Mama never came with us, but she was friendly to John and to Rose and all the other people, mostly men, who often came to our house.

John was a dressmaker, very expensive and very good. He sewed for a lot of rich people, and because he was a friend of Uncle Bunny, he made all of my going-out clothes and Mama's too.

Sunday evenings at Harbour View. I especially looked forward to the time when the sun set down slowly. The crickets could be heard and there was an extraordinary view of the sea from the balcony.

I spent a lot of time with Rose at Harbour View, talking about all sorts of things and admiring the view from the balcony, looking at the sky, sometimes red, other times blue and heavy with clouds. We were the only women at Harbour View and we would dance with the men and they with each other.

Rose was a kind woman, sweet and gentle. I enjoyed the times with her. I liked the smell of her perfume and to lose my head in her big bosom. She was John's assistant and helped him in his shop. I could see that she loved her brother madly by the way she talked to him and about him.

John was beautiful, his face long and angular without a trace of hair on it. He was light on his feet, so graceful when he walked and his clothes so colourful, I told myself that I would marry someone just like him.

I don't remember when our visits to Harbour View stopped. I remembered that Paul died and I never knew why because he seemed a healthy man. Rose visited us a few times and then she drifted away. Uncle Bunny still brought home Chin's Restaurant food, still had wonderful stories to tell, and we still cooked on Sundays. I still ironed Mama's hair and other men came over to visit.

We ate and danced at our house instead of Harbour View. But all this changed after Kevin came to live with us.

Kevin first moved in across the street from us to live with his uncle when I was thirteen and he was twenty. I first saw Kevin bending over the trunk of a Vauxhall car, pulling out pants length and folding them into a box. I later learned that with his uncle he sold the pants lengths to rural people, that he himself had come from St. Elizabeth to learn the trade. Kevin helped his uncle buy the cloth in town on the weekends, then took it to the county to sell. They were always talking about tyrleen and wool, tyrleen and wool. Seemed like that brand of cloth was a good buy.

Kevin and Uncle Bunny became friends and soon Kevin was coming over to our house for dinner and to sit on our verandah and talk. He seemed more like me than like an adult. I liked him even though he didn't have John's graceful moves or his talent. Kevin wasn't as lively as Uncle Bunny's other friends and his dress was a bit shabby, but he was devilish and I liked that.

I thought Mama liked him too because she would talk with him and Uncle Bunny until late at night. One of the things they talked about was Kevin and Uncle Bunny going into the cloth business together. Uncle Bunny was tired of Chin's Restaurant. After twenty-two years he wanted to try something new. He had saved up some money and wanted to go into his own business. Kevin was still working with his uncle so this planning was for the future.

Then Kevin moved in and shared Uncle Bunny's room. He began to take driving lessons that Uncle Bunny helped pay for. Sometimes we all went on the driving lessons, Uncle Bunny and I in the back seat, Kevin and the teacher in front. We all celebrated when Kevin got his license. Uncle Bunny brought home Chinese food and Mama baked a special cake.

Soon Kevin bought a car to take the pants lengths to the countryside to sell. He would leave on Wednesday morning and return on Saturday nights, full of long tales about his buyers at the market and about other vendors who couldn't compete with him. Business was a success and soon he and Uncle Bunny added shoes to their selection.

Kevin began dressing better and in more expensive pants and shirts. He even gained a bit of weight.

Sundays continued to be happy days. Sunday nights we piled into the car, Mama and I in the back, and went off to the drive-in movie theatre on Washington Boulevard. Close to the drive-in I would lay down on the floor of the car with Mama's foot over me and a sweater thrown carelessly on the other side to cover my head, my heart racing, wondering what would happen if the man who owned the drive-in searched the car, but giddy at the thought of getting into the movie for free. Uncle Bunny would pay the cashier for three adults and once we were safely inside the drive-in, I would rise from the floor to enjoy the movie and the pop corn and soda.

Things changed. Mama become quiet, almost withdrawn, and taken to drinking rum all the time. Days went by and we didn't see her except at night after the rum shops closed. Sometimes she would drink with G on the verandah. Uncle Bunny and Kevin spent more time alone together. When they were home they were always locked up in their room with the curtains drawn. Mama complained that the room was dark and musty and tried to get them out so she could clean.

Kevin hardly spoke to me any more. When he was in town he was usually out with Uncle Bunny, driving up and down. At times Mama wouldn't talk to them. I was afraid to ask Mama why and she never said a word to me. Mama and I started to spend our Friday and Saturday nights away from the house. She'd send me to Auntie Maggie's house or sometimes I'd go with her over to Auntie Maggie's bar. Mama no longer cooked for Uncle Bunny and Kevin.

Kevin stayed on in the house with Uncle Bunny, the two of them doing the things that Uncle Bunny and I used to do with John and Rose. But Kevin had other friends that he didn't bring home, mostly women.

Twice I overheard Uncle Bunny and Kevin arguing about Kevin's late nights. Some nights he did not come home until very late. Once I heard them arguing about a woman and a baby. I wondered why

Kevin wasn't living with the woman and the baby or how come he never brought her to the house.

One morning I awoke to loud voices in Uncle Bunny's locked room. For a moment I though he was fighting with Kevin again, but it was Mama yelling at Uncle Bunny that Kevin was only using him. Uncle Bunny would have none of that and he accused Mama of trying to come between them. The conversation ended abruptly with Mama coming out and slamming the door behind her.

I was asleep one morning when a hand on my breast made me jump up and scream. I saw Kevin running from my room, his back out the door before I was even fully awake. Had I not seen the back of his shirt, I would have been sure it was a dream. In a panic I rushed out to Mama. She held me in her arms tight as I told her what had happened, then she stormed into their bedroom, collared Kevin and threw him to the ground. I was sure she would kill him. I cried loudly, begging Mama to let him go. Kevin pushed Mama away and ran out of the house into his car.

We didn't see Kevin for two days. Uncle Bunny said it was probably a dream, or if it wasn't a dream, then Kevin was just playing. "Like a brother or cousin, he meant no harm". After that day Mama drank more and more and talked less and less.

I knew Mama had an older brother in Canada. We hadn't had much to do with him, but I knew his address. I wrote to him. I didn't mention what had happened to me, just about Mama's drinking and how lonely she was.

He wrote back to Mama immediately about getting us passports and bringing us to Canada. "Tell them you are coming up for a three-week visit. We will take care of the rest when you get up here."

Mama swore me to secrecy. "Don't tell Uncle Bunny a ting. Ah don't want dem to know. When yuh do dese tings, nobody should know, because it might backfire. Dis is just between mi and yuh."

Mama told Uncle Bunny a week before we were to board the plane to Canada. Auntie Maggie, countless cousins and Uncle Bunny came to the airport to see us off. I was dressed in a red dress that

John had made and red socks and I took the big thick sweater and woollen hat that Auntie Gwen had sent from England for me.

As we were going down the Palisadoes Road and past Harbour View I thought I saw the house with the view from the balcony onto the sea.

Remembering G

When I think back on my childhood G keeps coming
through: his musty clothes, the air around him heavy
with rum, stale tobacco smoke and furniture varnish.

Mama in front of the kerosene stove cooking dinner.
Mama in front of the wash tub, scrubbing board in her left
hand, khaki pants clutched in her right. Mama in front of the
Singer sewing machine, navy-blue-cloth-soon-to-be-school-
uniform in her lap. Mama in front of the kitchen counter,
turning flour and water into pastries...patties, plantain tarts,
totoes, gizzadas...Mama on the verandah, reading Harlequins,
Mama on the verandah reading the Gleaner.

Black mango, ginep, star apple, coconut water, guava,
sweetsop, neseberries, coolie plum and tinking toe, jimbling.

Cock crowing, children playing tug-o-war, the drop of a
breadfruit, mongrel dog Sammy jumping on the bitch's back
in broad daylight and she howling, St. Luke's church bells,

tamarind tree weeping in the wind. Black bat pitching on the wall. Man calling out, "Fresh snapper, parrot, jackfish fi sale." Woman with cotta and basket on head, she calling out "Buy me corn, 'ominy corn." Rain falling down on zinc roof and zinc fence. Monday drizzle mixed up wid dry dirt.

Sunflower, mango blossom, resurrection lily, shame-a-lady, spirit leaf.

Smells. Dead dog pon street, dead puss on side walk. Fried sprat, beef soup, rice and peas, curry goat, fried chicken, ox-tail and beans, corn meal and sweet potato pudding, steaming dukuno.

Ticks on dog....picking them and squashing them with a slipper. Lump in cornmeal porridge...and a beating if you don't eat it all off. Dog flea, dog bite. May Pen Cemetery, Chinese burial ground on Waltham Park Road, duppy, rolling calf, almshouse, madwoman, madman, John Crow eating dead dog, Madden's Funeral Home.

Long, lazy, childful days with Joy, Babes, Jackie, Gem, Lloydie, Tony, Gloria, Petal, Molly, Winnifred, Freddy, Elithia, Winsome, Pam, Winsome, Raymond, Rose.

Time mirroring the dead.

I see myself as a young girl, feeding the chickens, buying grass for the guinea pigs, cleaning my Oxford-brown shoes. Swinging on the thick rope hanging from the almond tree, high over the wire fence. And G coming with the wooden seat to fit into the rope. I remember him with joy and greediness. I was nine years old and he was forty.

G taking me to the rum shop. Telling the eager listeners, mostly men, that I was his youngest daughter. "Yes man, dis is mi baby. Youngest. Favourite." Telling his friends that he was married to

Mama. That his other children were in Canada, England and America. All lies, of course.

G taking me to buy ice cream and Archie comic books. Riding high on his back.

A make-believe world with white horses, carriages, valleys, mountains, steams, wide open spaces, quiet and peace.

I see G most everyday after school. The guinea pig pen is right next to the shed where he works. G is always working on something—a bedroom set, dining table with chairs or a cabinet for people's good dishes, cups and saucers, drinking glasses.

G is a carpenter. The best in Kingston, if not the whole island. He makes good money when he sells a piece of furniture. But he doesn't save. He doesn't believe in rainy days. G lives for now. Doing enough work to buy the next bottle of white rum and to buy me ice cream and Archie comic books. My G is a handsome man, tall, Black, and charming, smooth and sweet, like guava jam.

G likes to boast. He always does. He tells little lies too, which I keep secret from Mama. When G takes me out to get ice cream and we stop at a bar he always tells his friends and the barmaid that I am his daughter, that he is married to Mama, that he owns the house we live in on our little avenue. I keep his secret. I don't tell him that I know it's a secret. We don't talk about it, we just know.

I know Mama knows too. People come back and tell her, but she just sucks her teeth and says, "Talk is cheap. Mek him talk. Dose who know better know, dose who like gossip and kas kas will listen and believe, no matter what de truth." Then Mama just keeps on doing whatever it is that she is doing. The odd time she would curse G. "See here man, leave mi name alone, how yuh so wutliss. Is mi alone and God work for what I have, how yuh come into dis?" And she would walk off, not giving G a chance to defend himself.

G is helpful to Mama. He keeps her company. He runs errands for Mama. He cleans up the yard. He mends the roof when it leaks, he fixes odds and ends. Mama rents him the shed in the back to make his furniture and to meet his customers, but he hardly pays rent, even though Mama says that was the deal. She never harasses him because he is good company and he drinks rum with her. But he never sleeps in our house. Once he took me to a room in a tenement yard where he said he lived. Many nights G slept in our shed where he worked—on old clothes, sheltered by the zinc roof and hidden from the other tenants who lived in our yard by the guinea pig coop, the fowl coop and the unfinished furniture stacked in front of the shed.

G got up early on these mornings and started work on his furniture, whistling a song and pretending that he had just arrived for work.

Sometimes I would not see G for weeks at a time, for it was a regular habit of his to take his customer's money to buy wood and other supplies for making furniture and then disappear. There would be talk of him sitting stiff stone drunk in a bar, philosophising about Jamaica, about the federation, about our impending independence from Britain. The shed is where he comes back to when all the money run out. Staggering the length of Waltham Park Road until he reached our avenue and the concrete ground of the shed.

Here he sleeps off the rum.

"Mi little one," he greets me the next morning. "Ah busy, busy. Trying to work on big deals, big deals wid big money for some rich people up on de hills." He pauses and sucks on his tobacco, smoke pouring out of his nose. He waits for my response. That's what I like about G, he treats me like an adult.

"Yuh is de best carpenter in de land," I boast, "what de big people want yuh fi do?"

"Dem want mi to build a house, dem want mi to control de supervision. A lot of money dat, little one. When ah finish wid dat deal, den ah can concentrate on my house. Lots of land, up on de blue mountains, wid rivers and streams running tru, whole heap a bush, and quiet."

G's eyes get red and watery as he talks. If I didn't know better, I'd think it's because he's thinking about his dream house. But I know it's the rum and tobacco that does that to his eyes. "De only sound we'll hear is de crickets, peeny wallies and de beautiful sound of de doctor bird. But dis is our secret. Don't tell Mama. Ah want to surprise her." I promise. I'm imagining my own room and the river and bush and trees and birds and cricket sounds.

Mama is at the step of the shed. She sucks her teeth and her face is set up, so I know that she overheard G's secret. She hands G a plate of food and a cup of green tea.

"Thank yuh LuLu..." But before he can get another word in, Mama cuts him off.

"Look, stop tell dis pickney lie. Yuh is a good fi notten man."

"Blasted wutliss man! Weh yuh deh fi all dese weeks. Weh mi rent money fi de shed?" Mama doesn't wait for an answer.

"Mi nuh waan fi answer mi gate again to yuh customers. And is since when me tun yuh wife? Yuh love fi tek liberty wid mi nuh? Mi look like idiot?" She doesn't expect or want an answer from G. She goes on and on until she has the attention of all the tenants in our yard and Joy's mother next door.

"But Lulu, a...." Every time G tries to answer Mama cuts him off.

"Yuh not tired of dis kind of life? Yuh know how much people come to de gate knocking it down, asking for yuh, and waan to know how come yuh run off wid dem money? What ah must tell dem? Seh me and yuh married?"

This time Mama is waiting for an answer, but G is not bothering to take Mama on. G is concentrating on the green bananas, boiled dumplings and mackerel in his plate.

"Jus' tell yuh blasted customers, yuh don't live here. Don't run weh wid dem money and mek dem come here and try tek liberty wid me." With that last remark, she walks off, tired but satisfied.

G looks at me sheepishly. The silence is broken only by the singing of Joy's mother, who makes it her business to listen to anything that don't concern her.

"G, don't worry, your secret safe wid me, and ah don't tink Mama hear." I hug him tight and smell stale rum on his breath, his clothes musty smelling like a whole week without a bath, but that doesn't bother me.

"G, tell me more about dis dream house dat you going to build fi we in de middle of de blue mountains." But G is in a different mood now and doesn't want to talk.

"Not now, little one, ah have work fi do". "Can't yuh talk and work?" "No little one, we will talk anodder time."

"Mi can watch yuh work den?" I know his answer but I like to hear him say it.

"Fi mi little one, anyting." Then he lifts me off my feet and throws me high and before I realize I'm in air, I'm on the ground once again, standing tall.

I love to watch G work. Big black hands, veins as thick as rope threatening to burst free. The pencil behind the ear and two big lines across his forehead tells me he's concentrating. G sucks into his tobacco and a cloud of smoke pours out of his nose and all over his face. I run up to catch some of the smoke and almost choke.

The sound of the big wood cutting machine blocks out the chatter of the fowls and guinea pigs and the dog Sammy, who is running around howling. The lines on G's forehead are straight and precise, just like the wood he is cutting on the big machine.

G works like this for days. He is in the shed till late at nights sawing and planing big pieces of wood on different machines. Hammering and nailing. The nails are all sizes, some so tiny it's hard to imagine the face of the hammer pounding them without shattering them. Others so big that I wonder if they will split the wood. His clothes gets mustier with the smell of sweat.Perspiration stains are all over his shirt, but that can't keep me away from the shed.

G is in good spirits. He is working on a bedroom set for a lady. "Dis almost finish, little one. A few more touches, varnish and den a good polish wid dis rag, den to town we go."

He steps back often to look at the three pieces of furniture. A huge bed made out of mahogany wood, the dresser to match with a mirror and a stool to go with it. He's sanding down the sides of the bed.

"Got to get all de rough edges out of dis wood, de sandpaper mek it all smooth, so when a put de varnish on, it come up looking shine."

Then his voice is gay and proud. "So little one, what yuh want from town?"

"Ribbons, ribbons fi mi hair." I say, brushing back my two pig tails with the back of my hand, pretending my hair is long, long on my back, past my behind.

"Ribbons, ribbons, you shall have" says G, bowing before me like I am a princess.

"And colours, madam? What colours does de miss desire?"

"Many different colours, enough to fill a whole room!"

G's mood changes again. "So what do yuh tink Mama would like?" he half whispers.

"A newspaper and a pack of cigarettes, of course. Dat is what ah get her every birtday."

G is laughing, bending over, heaving like he's out of breath from running. And he can't stop laughing.

"Why yuh laughing, G?"

"Ah mean someting big, little one—tings women like, jewellery, scarves, perfume, tings like dat."

"Ah don't know, G, Mama don't wear jewellery and mi never see her wid perfume."

He looks disappointed, so I try to think. But the only thing that keep coming up and up in my mind is Mama's rent money for the shed and G is saying nothing about that, so I decide that I better leave that alone. That was big people business, between G and Mama.

"G, Mama wear Pond's powder on her face. We can get her dat and a scarf from Woolworth's store." G smiles and I am glad I said the right thing.

I didn't know for sure how much money G would be getting for the bedroom set. It seemed like an awful lot. I remembered G explaining to me that mahogany was a very expensive wood. "Yuh see this wood little one, a beauty to work wid. Ah wouldn't mind working in dis every day, but it is expensive and not everybody can afford dis kind to mek furniture."

He paused. "But money people—when yuh got money, it seem like it can buy everyting...but is not true little one, it cyaan buy freedom, it cyaan buy true independence and integrity...but dere is tings it can buy."

I nod, for I'm used to G talking like this, especially when he drinks, though he hasn't taken a sip of rum for many weeks.

I didn't go back to the shed for over a week. Mama's orders. I had to study hard for my school exams. I didn't even get a peep in the shed when I fed the guinea pigs and fowls, for Mama stood watching.

My exams passed and Friday came. I was free to spend time with G in the shed again. Four strangers were inside. I recognized the lady as G's customer: she was well dressed and even had stockings and high heels on, a white blouse and navy blue skirt. She looked like an office lady. The man beside her with hands in his pocket looked like her husband and was also neatly dressed. The other two men looked like the men G drank with in the rum shop, but I didn't know them. I was in time to see G uncover the bedroom set. Everyone stood silent, like the time Mama and I went to see a statue of a national hero unveiled. I watched the lady, her face looking as if a duppy just pass by her and she is in shock because she can't believe it and the duppy gone and she can't tell anybody because they will say she lie.

Her voice comes to her, "But man, yuh getting better and better all de time, dis piece of work is magnificent. Courts Furniture Store and dose places have notten over yuh. I can't understand why dem not ordering from yuh, but fi dem folly is fi mi good luck."

She laughs and turns to the man that came with her. He's just nodding and saying "Good work man, good work." I'm at the side looking on proudly, Mama beside me, and Joy's fass mother and a few other people trying to catch a peep through the zinc fence.

"What craftsmanship," the money lady went on, her voice like a radio announcer. She signals for the other two men. They knew exactly what was expected of them without her saying and lifted the pieces of furniture into a big truck parked outside our gate. There is a blue Austin car parked next to it. People from houses on our avenue are catching a look at G's furniture. Jackie comes out of her house to look. I climb over the fence and stand with her looking at the beautiful, polished furniture, but impatient to get back to the shed, I leave her standing.

The lady pays G and he smiles, showing tobacco-stained teeth. I know he's satisfied with the money because he is talking so fast that it's hard even for me to follow his words.

"Yuh tink yuh can make dis?" the lady asks, "Mi sister send dis magazine from England and ah like dis cabinet. Ah need a good looking and modern one like dis to put mi new dishes and glasses in."

G looked at the picture for a long while. Then he smiled again, "Yes it look like something ah can handle. A lot of intricate work though, it going to tek time, but is nothing ah can't do."

"Ah know dat. Dat is why ah come to you."

G is folding the paper from the magazine. "No, no, give dat to mi. Ah sure yuh memorize it and if yuh forget, come to mi house and have anodder look, but ah not leaving it wid yuh. Next ting yuh other customers come and see it and waan furniture looking like dis for dem house. No, no."

This time the money lady don't sound like one of those ladies on the radio reading the news or like an office lady. Now she sounds like somebody who lives on our avenue.

G is laughing again, "Mi regular customers couldn't pay fi dis kind of work Misses, so yuh don't haffi worry bout dat. Is more yuh friends who will want furniture like dat, so mi advise yuh to hide it away when yuh go home, so dem won't see it when dem come to visit." He laughs louder, enjoying his joke.

G told the lady that he wanted a down payment for the new cabinet he was about to make, but she wouldn't agree to it. "No, yuh start it and den come to me for money. Yuh know where I work. What yuh going to do with all dis money?"

She didn't wait for an answer but told him to call her when he was in the middle of the work. Had it been anyone else, I swear G would have told them to go to hell, but this lady was a respected customer and a reliable one. She also knew his weakness—his "ways," as he preferred to call his drinking periods.

The lady left.

G said he had some errands to do. Bills to be taken care of. But first he needed a shower and fresh clothes. Then he would take me to go shopping. G showered in the outdoor shower post and took a change of fresh clothes from a cardboard box in the shed close to the corner where he slept. Clean underpants, trousers, a short-sleeved shirt the colour of peach and clean black socks. He gave me his black and white shoes to polish with vaseline. G shaved off his moustache and beard in a cracked mirror that hung on one wall of the shed and splashed his face with Old Spice lotion. Mama came to the shed to join me as G was combing his hair. He greased it generously from a container of vaseline and used an old brush to encourage his hair to relax and lay flat like Mama's, which was straightened and pulled back.

Mama looked him up and down approvingly. "Yuh look nice. Not seeing yuh for the next couple days and nights." she teased.

"Ah coming back later after ah look about some bills to take dis little one shopping."

"Man yuh nuh tired fi tell lie, coming back when? Don't full up her head wid promises and dreams. Leave her mind free to remember de good times, don't bodder tell her foolishness."

G didn't answer Mama, but he winked at me and promised he would come back to take me to downtown Parade to shop for ribbons and other gifts.

G was ready to go. Washed and cleaned, he walked down our avenue turning left and right, greeting friends until he reached his first stop, the rum shop. I didn't see G again that evening. I held on tight to my disappointment, not sharing it with Mama. I didn't want to hear, "I told yuh so. Dat man is a disappointment, 'im wutliss." Early Saturday afternoon G came to get me. I had not expected him. He sat on the verandah talking with Mama—she as usual, cursing him for his unreliability and worthlessness—while I got dressed.

None of this mattered to me. G was just G.

We left the yard with Mama bidding us goodbye at the gate. Our first stop was Miss Olive's Bar on Waltham Park Road, across the street from the bus route that would take us downtown to Parade.

He was greeted generously. Most of the men in the bar had heard about the bedroom set.

Joy's father was the first to greet him, beckoning him to join his table. G waved him off, telling him, "Later," and sat down at the bar stool to talk with Miss Olive.

"Mek quite a bit of money on dis set, and mi have orders fi a lot more," he told Miss Olive. "Pass me a drink of de whites and give mi little daughter here a soda pop."

Miss Olive, who had a sweet spot for G and his money, encouraged him to talk more. She was a red-skinned lady, with lots of hair on her head. Much more than Mama. She was broad just like Mama and the same height.

"So Mr. Big Man, buy mi table a drink nuh?" shouted Joy's father from a table in the corner. He knew exactly how to catch G's attention: he liked to be called Big Man and Mister.

"Olive, serve dem each a round of white rum fi me, and just put it on mi tab."

After my fourth bottle of soft drink and with my belly feeling like an overblown balloon, I begged G to let us go. He told Miss Olive to keep the tab and we headed across the street to catch the bus.

On a Saturday evening downtown Kingston is like a great big carnival. People on the street, car horns blowing non-stop, loud music, vendors on sidewalks selling shoes, cloth, ribbons, hair clips, candies. The market around the corner with fruits and vegetables. The big stores down on King Street, selling more cloth and shoes. Woolworth's, jewellery stores, toy shops, book shops, banks. More street vendors selling ice cream, snow cones, patties, cakes—all the way to the waterfront where we visit the Craft market.

The first place we stop is Woolworth's to get Mama her face powder, a box of seven handkerchiefs with an embroidered flower on each for the different days of the week and a yellow and blue scarf. The store is very crowded and I hold on tight to G's hand. The last thing we buy is my ribbons, a variety of colours. Then back out on the street.

The side walks are crammed and boys in short pants with the backsides torn out are running up and down barefoot. G tells me to be careful with my little change purse because there are many pick-pockets downtown. G, tall and handsome, holding my hand. There's a Rastaman, barefoot with dreadlocks way down his back, selling brooms. "See dat man", says G, "dem call him Bongo dread. He's a peaceful Rastaman, not like some of dem other ones." We pass the Rastaman selling his brooms; he looks fierce with his long locks, some have turned red and are sticking up all over his head. We buy more ribbons for my hair from a sidewalk stall. Vendors everywhere. "Coconut water fi sale, little girl. Yuh nuh thirsty, get your nice father to buy yuh one," shouts a man with a handcart full of coconuts. G asks if I want. I say yes and he stops to buy. We have three coconut trees in our yard, but standing there on King Street in my going-out clothes, holding a coconut to my head, feels bold and risky. The man cuts the coconut down the middle and hands it back to me. I eat the insides, white and sweet.

We continue down King Street, I'm holding tight to G's hand and skipping when the crowd is not too thick. We pass another Rastaman, sitting on the concrete ground against a store and reading a passage from the Bible. I don't know which passage, but I have heard it before. He is loud, but he's not reading to anyone in particular. "Yuh see dat one," G says, "him mad, smoke too much ganja." He doesn't seem mad to me. He's reading the same Bible scripture that I hear in church. His eyes are red like G's, his clothes soiled, a bit like how G looks when he hasn't bathed for a long time. He pays us no attention. As we get closer to where he's sitting I pull on G's hand to slow down. He looks fiercer than the first one with the brooms and he starts talking to me.

"Know who de true and living God is. Dere is no heaven up dere in de sky, yuh have fi find it right here on earth among de heathens and parasites." G is pulling me away, but I hold fast to the sidewalk. The Rastaman continues. "Read yuh Bible, know it, don't learn it. Knowing is true wisdom". People crowd the sidewalk, his voice is harsh as he addresses us. "To de chief Musician, a Psalm or Song of David: 'Let God arise, let 'is enemies be scattered/ Let dem also dat hate 'im flee before 'im/ As smoke is driven away, so drive dem away/ As wax melteth before de fire, so let de wicked perish at de presence of God.' "

His eyes getting redder, his locks thick like the rope I swing on. He wets his lips, pauses, looks around at the crowd and continues: "Sing unto God, sing praises to 'is name/ Extol 'im dat rideth upon de heavens/ by 'is name JAH and rejoice before 'im."

We all stand there, not moving. Even G cannot pull himself away.

The sun is still hot. Even with the random breeze coming from the sea we are both sweating. I like to sit here and watch the sea, not minding the stench from the water riding in on the breeze. The sea stretches blue-green, endless, waves roaring. We find a bench close by to rest our feet, but no sooner than we sit, G tells me that he's thirsty. I promise to sit and wait until he comes back.

My arm is wet with heat, sweat washing my back, I pretend it's sea water, cool and green. Three boys my age and a man and lady walk by. I know they're not from here. The boys are dressed in white socks, blue shorts and white T-shirts. One calls the man "daddy" in a funny-sounding voice; it must be American or Canadian because they don't sound like they're from England. They are excited by the sight of the water, and want to know if they can go in and swim. Silly white boys, don't they know the water is dirty? Don't they know nobody swims on this side, don't they know that you don't come to downtown Parade to swim?

A crowd is gathering away from me, shouting, laughing and an occasional cuss word, and the slapping down of something that sounds like dice. G is taking a long time. I'm hot and bored. Flies dart at my face. I head towards the crowd. Four men are sitting on oil drums. A board is spread across the middle. Dominoes slap down on the board. The men are laughing and drinking beer.

Suddenly the laughter stops. The man sitting closest to where I am standing has a knife at the throat of a man who had been standing behind him. "How much time ah tell yuh don't blood-claat stan' up behind mi and give out mi hand? Yuh want to dead bwoy?" The one with the knife at his throat protests. But the other is angry and pushes the knife in a little. "So what mi is, a liar? Mi blind? Bwoy, a years and years mi a play domino, yuh know." The game breaks up and the board is on the ground, dominoes all over the street. More men get mixed up in the quarrel. Now someone tries to get the knife. Clouds of angry words back and forth. "Let go mi rass-claat knife."

"Rest and settle. Yuh want police come down on us? Rest de bwoy, 'im nuh worth it," says one of the men who were watching game. He had a multi-coloured tam on his head. I am frightened, but I don't know how to move away. There is blood, red, red on the pavement.

"Fuck off," someone shouts. Stones and tin cans are flying over my head. I don't want to cry, but I'm frightened. I'm biting my nails, the skin underneath them is bleeding too. Someone pulls my hand, "Little one, dis is no place fi yuh. Come to G, let we get out of here, poor baby." Five police cars pull up and policemen rush out, guns in hand. Someone in the crowd shouts, "Rahtid, de war start now."

The bus takes us back to our neighbourhood. The sun is almost gone. We stop at Miss Olive's.

"Yes, boss man. Buy we a drink nuh?" G recognizes the man, sitting with two ladies, and asks Miss Olive to serve them. He buys a drink for himself too. A soda and patty for me.

"Come join we nuh money man." Six rounds later G has forgotten about taking me home. I'm not frightened though. Miss Olive knows Mama and I know a lot of the people in the bar. It's noisy and from time to time I hear cuss words, but I don't mind. G has given me money to play the jukebox all night if I want.

"I have so much work coming in," I hear G say, "can't handle it all. Soon mi will haffi open a big operation and employ bout a dozen man fi help mi." If the men knew he was lying, they make no sign. They were willing to listen to story tellers, philosophers, amateur politicians so long as the drinks were free. The night staggers on. I play almost every song in the box, my stomach fat with soda pop, G deep into his stories.

Three more men join the table. One I know, a brown-skinned man, Mr. Minor, well respected in our neighbourhood. I don't know where he works. But he is about the only man in our neighbourhood who wears a tie and white shirt to work. Now the talk is about Jamaica's independence, corruption in political parties and why common people like G and others aren't hired on government jobs. I've heard all of this before.

G's story is well underway. "Yes man, ah really suffer under dis government. Can't figet dem. When time come to vote dem all over yuh and when dem in dem figet yuh. Mi use to have a good job working on de university building, at Mona Campus, working on a new design, changing de roofs over to flat roofs, good pay. I work hard and steady."

G stops and takes a sip of his drink. "Den one day de contractor come and tell mi dat whole heap of men out of job, and dese men had supported de new government in power and voted for dat government. Said dem like how mi work, but dem getting pressure from people up at de top to let mi go." He takes another sip, satisfied that he has a big audience. G knows a lot of people and they know of his work.

"But mi don't support any of dem. Not me. Dem can't buy mi. Mi bigger dan dat." His voice is getting higher now and he is waving his hands at Miss Olive to bring more drinks for the men. "Mi not saying ah radical or revolutionary, yuh know. Mi just a simple man. All ah want to do is to drink mi waters, have food to eat, a place to sleep, and mi willing to work fi dat. But ah cyaan support corruption."

Mr. Minor cut in. "But hold it, yuh cyaan just ignore dis political process no matter how corrupt it is. We still haffi vote. Some countries man don't even have vote. How yuh expect to better yuhself man, yuh nah deal wid reality." He snickers, looks around the bar and continues, "Now look, if saltish scarce and yuh want it, yuh have to know de storekeeper, de storekeeper most likely defend one of de parties, and de storekeeper going to sell de fish to dat customer who defend dat party because de storekeeper buy it from a bigger man who in dat same party. So how yuh going to eat?"

"How yuh going to work? How yuh familly going to benefit?" The men around start to see Mr. Minor's point and begin nodding their heads in agreement. "How yuh can start yuh own business? Weh yuh going to get lumber to buy? Weh yuh going to get credit? How yuh going to be successful if yuh nuh support a political party?"

G is not about to be outdone. "Any a yuh get any big job after de election?. Answer nuh? Who get big job? Right. None a we. Whether we vote or not dem already have dere people pick out. So what we going to be satisfied with? One piece a saltish and a pound a flour?" The men are now nodding in agreement with G. It's late and the bar is noisier and more crowded, Miss Olive asks G, "Why yuh nuh take de child home? It too late for her. Take her home and come back."

"One more round for everybody and mi will tek her home." G is about to continue talking, when in walks a big-belly policeman, a regular in our neighbourhood. Not many people like him. He was a showoff and the rumour was that he jailed and beat up men for very little reason and got away with it because of his connection to the party in power.

He looks around, nods and orders a double scotch with water on the side. It was known that he drank a lot, ordered the most expensive drinks and never paid for them. Even Miss Olive, who could tackle almost anyone who didn't want to pay up, did not tangle with him. The men at G's table changed the conversation to the day's horse racing at Caymans Park. The big-belly policeman is trying to feel up Miss Olive's behind. She pushes his hands away firmly, but she is laughing and whispering something to him. G watches. I know he is sweet on Miss Olive and doesn't like what the policeman is doing. He knows that if Miss Olive curses the policeman out, he will bring her up on charges for entertaining illegal gambling in her back room, despite the fact that he plays there all the time and wins lots of money. Everybody in the neighbourhood knows this. "Come on, little one, mek we go home."

Mama is waiting for us. There is no smile on her face. I look at G's face. He's looking at Mama, as if bringing me home past midnight is the most natural thing in the world. "Lulu, we had a good time, look we even buy presents fi yuh. Little one, show Mama her gifts and yuh ribbons and pretty hair clips."

Mama already has her speech prepared. "Yuh is a madman or what? Is since before lunch time yuh have dis pickney out on de street and yuh just coming back wid her. Yuh mad or what? No, yuh nuh mad, yuh drunk and is de last time yuh tek mi pickney out of dis yard."

"Okay darling, ok mi honey, let's don't fight. It is such a beautiful night." G coaxes.

"Just move yuhself, bout darling. Yuh only care bout one ting—yuh liquor." Mama holds me tight, turning me around and around till I am dizzy. "Let me look at yuh child, let me see if yuh still in one piece." She holds me tight and sends me off to bed. I fall asleep long before Mama comes in.

I'm up early the next morning, thinking about my day with G. The shopping downtown, the fight, Miss Olive's bar, about Mama and G.

It's three weeks now and G hasn't come around. I go to the shed everyday after school, but it's empty. Mama says I shouldn't worry, that's the way G is. Mama sometimes acts as if she doesn't really like G, the way she talks about him.

A woman came to the gate yesterday, demanding to see G, said he took her money for work and she hasn't seen the work or him since that day. She didn't believe Mama, so Mama, full contempt showing on her face, opened the gate wide and invited the woman to search the shed. The woman boldly came in and looked from corner to corner and then left with a trail of cuss words behind her.

Today when I go to the shop for Mama to buy her newspaper, I will go over to Miss Olive Bar to ask about G. Miss Olive says G came in two weeks ago but she hasn't seen or heard from him since.

I go to school, feed the guinea pigs and fowls, play with my friends. Swinging high on my swing, I look up the avenue for some sign of G. But there is none.

A boy is banging at the gate with a stone. Mama breathes a heavy sigh and mumbles, more to herself than me, "Dat blasted man. Ah sure is somebody else come bout dem money and furniture." Mama sends me to the gate. The boy sees me coming, but he is still banging hard. The dogs are yelling, racing ahead of me, ready to tear him up, a john crow is circling another dog, dead for three days out on the street. Half of the insides already gone, picked out by the likes of this crow and family. I hold my nose as I approach the gate.

"What yuh want?" I am impatient and rude. He is equally so. "Mi waan fi talk to a big 'oman, not yuh," he says, looking me up and down as if he were a big man. "Mi looking for a Miss Lulu." I motion for Mama to come to the gate. "Mek him come in," Mama shouts.

Although the boy is acting so mannish, I see he is terrified of the dogs, barking and jumping as if they had not eaten in days.

"Is ah-right," I reassure him. "Dem won't bite yuh, all bark and no bite, like some people." I hold on to the necks of both dogs and the boy runs up to the verandah.

"Ah come for a Mr. G. 'Im is in de Kingston Public Hospital." Mama stands there as if the boy has said that G is around the corner having a drink.

Imagining all kinds of things, I sit down hard on a chair, afraid

I'm going to faint. "What him doing dere?" I ask loudly, before Mama can speak. The boy ignores me. "Talk nuh man, yuh never come wid a message?" Mama asks. "Yes mam, five nights ago him fall in de big gully off Waltham Park Road. Him buss 'im head...unconscious fi days and couldn't talk and didn't have no identification on 'im. But dis morning he start fe talk a little and he said dis is weh him live and to ask fi yuh." Mama is now smoking a cigarette.

My heart is going so fast I am afraid to talk in case it jumps out of my mouth. I know the gully. I use it, unknown to Mama, when taking short cuts from school. The boys play marbles in it and after a heavy rain storm, we all make paper boats and sail them in the gully. But it's no place for a drunk man to walk through. At night not even a brilliant moon can guide a sober man, much less a drunk man. The gully has a lot of curves, some of the concrete worn off by heavy rains, and it has some sharp surprise edges, where you can fall into the gutter.

The boy is shuffling from one foot to the other. Mama is smoking calmly, not saying anything. "Well, mi going now," he says. He looks at me. "Can yuh follow me out to de gate and hold yuh dogs?" I have no energy to hold the dogs, so I pick up a big stick and wave it towards them. The boy moves towards the gate and the growling starts. I shout at the dogs to shut up and wave the stick closer to them, hitting Sammy on his back. He lets out a loud yelp and runs off behind the house. The other one lays low. At the gate I ask the boy, "How mi cyan find 'im if me a go to Public Hospital?" He hurriedly tells me, grateful to be out of the yard and away from the dogs.

"Let mi just tell yuh someting before yuh open yuh mouth," Mama greets me. "Mi not going to visit dat wutliss man." She goes on and on, and I am crying, sure my heart is going to burst open my chest.

I woke up later that afternoon on the couch with a blanket over me. Mama was there beside me with a bowl of soup. "Tomorrow," she said softly, patting my head, "yuh can go and see G. Mi will cook some chicken soup fi yuh to carry — ah sure dem starving 'im down dere — dat place is not fit for a dead dog."

G's head is covered in bandages. I can barely see his eyebrows. He looks rested. Tears jump out of my eyes. I am so glad to see him that I try not to cry. We hug each other for a long time and then I sit on the side of his bed for my visit. He introduces me as his daughter, then drinks the chicken soup as the other men—six or seven of them, look on enviously. The room is much too small for so many people. G says they will discharge him in a few days because they need the bed space. I stayed with him a long time and left only when the sun went down.

G is in the shed. He came here straight from the hospital. I told him he should be home resting, but he insisted he had too much work to finish up and could not think about himself. Mama is kind to him. She offers him a plate of food and a glass of sweet drink. She asks about his head and reminds him to keep his appointment for his checkup.

Every chance I get I am in the shed with G. I hardly play with my friends anymore. G is working hard to complete all the work he has promised his angry customers. There is a big old arm chair in the shed and I sit there, reading my comic books and listening to the sounds of the tools that G uses to make furniture. It seems like G has been out of the hospital for a long time, but he still has his head bandaged. He hasn't been to Miss Olive's Bar since his accident. His hands, so rough from sandpaper, turpentine, glue, are perfectly precise, hammering the tiniest nails into the wood.

G's friends from Miss Olive's Bar come to see him often and each time they bring a flask of rum. The conversation is always the same: the past election, dead federation, corruption. There is always a philosopher, political analyst and storyteller in the crowd. G's position always the same. "Voting achieves notten. Dem jus' did pull de wool over we eyes. Democracy is a hoax."

Another man comes in with more rum and the conversations continues. Joy follows her father into the shed and I make room for her on my chair. A few other kids are hanging around with their fathers or uncles. The conversation changes briefly to pick-a-pow and drop-hand. Joy's father is telling the men that he won today. "Today is mi lucky day. Ah wake dis morning and ah say to Joy mother, yuh know, Enid, today is mi lucky day. Ah going down to de Chinese shop to bet on number ten, and it come in." A younger man asked him how he knew ten was a winning number.

"Mi never know, but ah had a dream last night, bout dogs and some other tings a can't even 'member, so ah decide to bet on dog, and ah know dog is number ten." The young man wanted to ask more questions, but he was cut off by one of the men from Miss Olive's Bar. "Buy us a drink den. Share yuh good fortune wid us." The younger man was sent to make the purchase and I to get more ice and water from Mama's fridge.

"Wonder what dis independence ting will mean?" one of the men asked. "Should open up lots of opportunities fi we, more rights for Black man, we will be leaders of our own house." Without looking up from my comic book I knew it was Mr. Minor. G sucks his teeth, pulls on his tobacco and looks around at the other men before addressing Mr. Minor. "Yuh really believe dat? Not in our lifetime. Black man time won't come wid independence. We will still be behind de white man, den de brown man." His voice was rising now. "Independence won't do anyting fi de Black man, he will have to do it fi himself. And fight like hell, fight de white man who now mek here 'im home and de brown man who don't want to be black. Independence won't help dis little one here," pointing at me. "Independence won't help dem here," motioning to the other kids sitting on the ground. "Independence won't help de conditions in de Public Hospital, wid two people to one bed. Independence won't tell we pickney dem dat de sky is de limit, it won't fill dem head wid dreams and possibilities. We haffi control we own destiny and we won't from a piece of paper dem gi wi, saying wi now independent." Satisfied, he turned to Mr. Minor. "What yuh got to say bout all dat?"

Mama calls out for me to bathe.

Since early today people were moving furniture from the shed, work that G completed, to the relief of his customers. Even the uptown money lady came with her husband and the two men to pick up her cabinet for her expensive glasses and dishes. Our yard is crowded with people admiring G's craftsmanship. He was as proud as ever. G left with the van that carried the cabinet. He waved to me, promising to come back soon.

G has disappeared again.

Five days gone and no sign of G.
I sit and wait in the old arm chair.
They found him.
In the gully
Cracked skull.
Broken neck.
Time mirroring the dead.

Memory

Every now and then G comes to mind.
The avenue.
Childhood friends.
The house with the balcony looking on to the sea.
Zinc fence.
Rusty zinc pan.
Mongrel dog Sammy.

There are no balconies here.
The verandas are not as big and wide.
No wooden floor with fretwork designs.
No rain beating down on zinc roof.

No dogs running free. No cows on the loose.
Squirrels and raccoons running free.
Dogs on leash. Cats on leash.

Ice and cold.
Sun and Hot.
Snow
Blizzard
Bald-headed trees.
Dead Leaves

School yard. Trains. Shopping centres.
White, white, white all around.
No longer forced to recite Longfellow.
No longer shamed into remembering the date Christopher
Columbus "discovered" Jamaica.
Time to forget the names of his three ships.
History class is about the English and the French.
History is about the "discovery" of North America by Christopher
Columbus.
History is Canada's Indians on reserves.
Hudson Bay Company.

School yard chants
Nigger
Darkie
Negro
Chocolate face
Nigger

Time mirroring the dead.

Dead
fades
time

But every now and then
When the cold tears away at my soul
Joints cold and cracked

The view of the sea off the balcony rescues me.

It is not good to travel today
Neither to cross the ocean
Deserts so dry, water thirst will
Kill yuh, kill yuh

When it wet it slippery yeah
When it damp it cramp yuh belly
Don't want to see you on de ground
Caution take heed - Black Soul
  Burning Spear - "Black Soul"

Glossary

a - is, be, am, are, it, is, there, are, to, of, in, at.

ackee - a fruit tree. The edible flesh of this fruit is often eaten with saltfish. This plant as brought here in a slave ship from the coast of Africa.

ah - I.

Anancy - a trickster, the spider hero of traditional Jamaica stories of Ashanti origin.

beg - ask.

blood-claat - in language of abuse usually refers to woman's sanitary towel.

bruk - break.

bruk-up - broken up.

bwoy - boy.

chile - a young person.

coolie gal - an East Indian girl. Formerly a neutral word, now used derogatively by many non-East Indians and objected to by East Indians. East Indians began coming to Jamaica as indentured labourers in 1834.

coolie plum - a fruit shaped like a very small apple.

cotta - a circular pad made of twisted cloth, placed on the head to protect it and to steady the load being carried.

cut-eye - To catch someone's eye and then quickly lower the eyelids while turning the head away. An insulting action or mark of scorn. (e.g; 'She cut her eye after me.')

cyaan - can't.

at - that.

dandy-shandy - in this context a ball game with three or more people in which one, at the shout 'dandy shandy', runs out of the line of a thrown ball.

dasheen - a ground provision. (e.g; yam, coco.)

deh - there.

dem - them, also used to indicate plural. (e.g; di keys dem -the keys.)

den - then.

dere - there.

dese - these.

dis - this.

dose - those.

Dreadlocks - a Rastafarian - the hair in dreadlocks is washed and grown uncombed.

dukuno - a kind of pudding made of some starch food (e.g; plantain, green banana, cassava flour, cornmeal) sweetened, spiced and usually wrapped in plantain or banana leaf, and boiled, baked or roasted.

duppy - ghost.

dutty - dirty.

dutty cloth - dirty cloth.

eh - asking for repetition of a statement or for agreement.

fass - interfering, meddlesome, quick to intrude in other's business.

fi - for, to.

'fore - before.

fried sprat - small fish fried crisply in hot coconut oil.

gal - girl.

ginep, ginep - a tiny green plum shaped fruit with a tough skin that grows in clusters on a very large tree.

gizzada - an open tart filled with grated, sweetened, and spiced coconut. Also called sweet-cake.

grater-cake - cakes made of grated coconut and unrefined 'wet' or 'new' sugar.

guava cheese - a conserve of guavas, strained and boiled down with sugar to a solid consistency, which may be sliced like cheese.

gwan - to go

haffi - have to.

hard-dough bread - unsliced bread with a crust.

jimbling (jimbelim, jimilin) - an extremely acid fruit, pale greenish - yellow, which comes out in clusters from the trunk and branches of the tree.

kas kas - to dispute, to quarrel.

mawga - thin, lean; by implication often underfed, half-starved.

mek - make.

mi - I, me, my.

mout - mouth.

naseberries (nisberry) - a fruit the size of a small apple covered with a rough brown coat, the inside of which is a succulent sweet pulp. It grows on a very tall tree.

nega (neyga) - a derogatory term used to describe Blacks, often implying 'extra' blackness, backwardness, and stupidity.

nottin - nothing.

nuff - enough.

nuh - doesn't.

nyam - to eat greedily.

'oman - woman.

'ominy corn - a drink. corn boiled and sweetened with condensed milk.

paradise plum - a sweet, a candy.

piazza - the colonnaded entryway to a shop shaded by a roof or a series side by side which form a covered walk for pedestrians.

picky-head - when a girl's hair grows close very short to the scalp - derogatory term referring to hair quality.

pickney - a child.

petchary bird - (pichieri) (pecheere) a bird. its belligerence and its habit of pursuing the John crow are noticed proverbially. it has a black head and long beak.

plantain tart - a Jamaican pastry made from plantain and flour.

'pon - at, upon, on.

rass-claat - a swear word often used in a exclamatory way to show strong opposition, scorn, anger, impatience.

resurection lily - a kind of lily which flowers on Good Friday and smells sweet after four o'clock.

rolling calf - a ghost, taking the form of a monster with fiery eyes, who trails a long chain behind it. People who lead dishonest or wicked lives are said to 'turn rolling calf' when they die.

sah - sir.

seh - say, that.

shame-alady - a flower. it is sometimes called, shame brown lady, shame bush, shamebush, shame lady, shame ol' lady. The slightest touch causes its leaflets to close.

spirit leaf - the common plant whose pods burst when wet.

star apple - a fruit. it is called 'star apple' because in the cross section it resembles a many pointed figure.

sweetsop - a sweet, succulent fruit alledgedly favoured by women.

tamarind - a bow shaped pod with seeds inside covered by tart brown flesh, which is often soaked and made as a drink.

tek - take.

tick - stick.

ting -thing.

tink - stink.

stinking toe - a bean like fruit resembling a large brown human toe and having an unpleasant odour.

thru pence - three pennies or a three penny piece.

unno - you (usually in the plural, sometimes in the singular.)

weh - which, what, whatever, where.

wid - with.

wutliss - worthless.

yard - the usual word for the land around a piece of property.

yuh - you, your, yours.

This glossary contains Jamaican words and English words with non-standard usages as they appear in the text. The spellings and interpretations owe a great deal to the *Dictionary of Jamaican English* edited by F.G. Cassidy & R.B. LePage (Cambridge University Press, London, 1967).